THE
EXECUTIVE
LOOK

THE EXECUTIVE LOOK

How to Get It—How to Keep It

MORTIMER LEVITT

New York ATHENEUM *1985*

Portions of this book in somewhat different form were published
as *The Executive Look and How to Get It,* An AMA Management Briefing,
by Mortimer Levitt, Copyright © 1979 by AMACOM, a division of
American Management Associations. All rights reserved.

Library of Congress Cataloging in Publication Data

Levitt, Mortimer, ———
    The executive look.

    1. Men's clothing.   2. Grooming for men.
I. Title.
TT618.L48   1981   646   80-66011
ISBN 0-689-11078-2

Published simultaneously in Canada by Collier Macmillan Canada, Inc.
Composition by American-Stratford Graphic Services, Inc., Brattleboro, Vermont
Manufactured by Halliday Litho, West Hanover, Massachusetts
Designed by Kathleen Carey
First Printing September 1981
Second Printing December 1981
Third Printing August 1982
Fourth Printing August 1984
Fifth Printing December 1985

———

FOR MIMI,

who added the fourth dimension to my life.

———

———

Acknowledgments

———

"Behind every good man there stands a better woman." In this instance, there were two. I want to acknowledge the help I received from Betty Vaughn and Katie Rawdon, two women who are so thoroughly professional that their careers would have been assured long before the term *women's liberation* was conceived. Without their persistent encouragement, this book might never have been written.

Contents

Contents

PART ONE

THE PROBLEM

*"Too Many Executives Fail to Project
an Image Appropriate to Their Chosen Careers"*

1

Why the Maitre D' Looks Better than the Man Tipping Him

HAVE you ever noticed that the maitre d' in a good restaurant often looks better than the man who tips him?

The reason is simple. The maitre d' is wearing professionally designed clothes—a uniform, really, whereas the patron, who could be the chief executive in a Fortune 500 company, or one of the young lions of his particular profession, wears whatever strikes his amateur's fancy. Ever since his mother stopped dressing him, our young businessman has been out to sea as far as clothes go. Although he may dress acceptably according to the standards of his peers, by and large he does not know why he wears what he wears, nor does he understand the various impressions—some good, some not so good—that his choice of clothes makes on colleagues and clients. Usually, he really doesn't care to think about it. The shirt and tie he received for Christmas may not go with the suit that was on sale the day he stopped by the village haberdasher—but that is the combination he arrives in for lunch at "21." And so it is that he is outshone by the very man who lives on his tips.

This book is written for the career-minded man who, like the gentleman above, projects an image that does not do justice to his social or intellectual standing, because he wears clothes according to happenstance, whim, cliché, myth, and habit. I propose to replace this chaotic approach to dress with a simpler and

3

The shirt and tie he received for Christmas may not go with the suit bought on sale.

sounder program based on guidelines developed in the course of four decades of literally making it my business to help men look as good as they are. My guidelines are easy to understand, inexpensive to apply, and in most cases, instantaneously effective. By following them, any intelligent man-on-the-move can quickly learn not only how to use his present clothes to best advantage, but also how to make additions that will give him a wardrobe that both complements his particular physical makeup and is appropriate to his professional situation.

The real beauty of my system, from the point of view of a genuinely busy man, is that once it is put into effect, very little time and thought are necessary to project consistently an image of substance.

As easy as my guidelines are to understand and to implement I have often encountered an obstinate attitude when trying to communicate them to friends. They seek my advice on investments and taxes, film and theater projects, tennis-court construction, sailboat racing, skiing, and a host of other areas in which I

4

have been active over the years. But about clothes, the one area where my expertise is unquestioned, they do not ask. The problem is that like most men, they are afraid of what a professional might say about their attire.

Occasionally, in utter frustration, I break my own rule of never forcing on a friend my opinion about appropriate dress. One night, for instance, I saw Brendan Gill, an old friend and favorite author, on a television talk show. Brendan is so articulate and engaging that usually it makes little difference what he wears, but on this particular evening his collar was one size too large and it made him look slightly ridiculous. The next day I sat down and wrote him a letter that began:

> I just can't stand it any longer. You are brilliant, charming, and distinguished. Unfortunately, you always look slightly tacky, like Bertrand Russell, etc.

I went on to offer him a gift of six choice-of-the-house shirts, custom-made to his individual measurements. Then I suggested he call my secretary to make an appointment with our chief designer.

Brendan's reply was immediate and favorable:

> "Oh, what a funny letter! It has kept me laughing all day and it has also given pleasure to many of my colleagues, who share your view of my sartorial disarray. Bless you, I will be so pleased to have real shirts at last. I'll follow your instructions and arrange to put the problem of my peculiar body at the disposal of your best orthopedic designer. . . ."

But despite two follow-up calls by my secretary, Brendan never showed up. The point of the story is that Brendan was paying the issue of his personal appearance lip service only.

Many of Brendan's peers feel pretty much the same about their appearance:

1. Walter Cronkite, who is relatively fastidious, sends his secretary over to pick out shirts and ties—all ready-made.
2. New York governor Hugh Carey regularly sent an aide to pick out his ready-made shirts, until we wrote saying that although

we were delighted to have him as a customer, our ready-made shirts did not fit him properly. He grudgingly took time out to be measured, then left the selection of fabrics to an aide.

3. New York mayor Ed Koch, a shirt-sleeve congressman if there ever was one, wore only popular-priced white shirts while serving in Washington. Because he is tall, his sleeves were too short and his shirttails were always inching out of his trousers. Like the late president Lyndon Johnson, Koch has a long neck, and the low collar of his ready-mades exposed wrinkles that were better covered. It was Bess Meyerson who insisted we take him in hand. He agreed reluctantly, but was delighted with the results. He now carefully selects the fabrics himself, and wonder of wonders, in January 1980 he was selected by the Institute of Fashion as one of the Ten Best Dressed Men of 1979.

4. Charles Revson, who singlehandedly created the Revlon cosmetics empire, was a forceful, creative genius who always dressed in a plain black suit, plain white shirt, and plain black tie. Revson

A career man should always look as good as he is—meeting or no meeting.

Charles Revson, Revlon's creative genius, wore only black tie, white shirt, and black suit to business—a case of arrested development.

borrowed the look from formal clothes because that's when he looked his best—Yet, it was really a case of arrested development. Creative as Revson was, he lacked the imagination to vary the look by including, for example, a black tie with white polka dots, or a plain navy suit, white shirt, and navy tie with white stripes. There are many possible variations on the same theme.

Even the most important of men *can* be educated to care about their appearance, as the following anecdote illustrates. Some years ago I received a letter from the White House accompanied by a blue pleated shirt to be worn with a tuxedo. The shirt came from President Johnson, who wanted it copied. I could see that the shirt would be totally unsatisfactory, since the collar was much too low, front and back, for the president's long neck and the sleeves obviously too short for such a tall man. Furthermore, blue was suitable only for appearances on T.V. I decided to send my chief designer, Jerry Efron, to the White House, and an appointment was arranged. A limousine met him at the airport, and he was taken directly into the president's bedroom. Efron showed President Johnson what was wrong with his shirt, took proper measurements, explained the principles of color coordination, and showed him how to knot a tie properly. The president then ordered thirty-three shirts, which Efron brought down two weeks later by "special executive order."

One night shortly thereafter, my daughter answered the telephone at home. She laughed and said, "Daddy, it's the White House"—and it was. The president had been trying to reach Efron (who had an unlisted telephone number), because he was going on national television the next night, and couldn't remember how to tie our special Custom Shop Knot. President Johnson actually wanted Efron to fly down and tie his tie for him! I thought this was carrying things too far, so I said that Efron was away and the president would look just fine.

He did. In fact, before the television address the next night, the CBS-TV announcer noted the change in the president's image: "The president looks like a new man. He's let his hair grow back to its natural gray color, and he is wearing a higher collar that makes him look younger, even though his hair is grayer." (That would have made a great Custom Shop commercial, if the announcer had known of our involvement.) So serious was the president about his new image that he actually telephoned Efron two days after the broadcast to ask, "How did I look? Do you have any further suggestions?"

Unfortunately, President Johnson was the proverbial exception to the rule. In my experience, only two groups of men care very much about the way they look. The first group consists of recent immigrants to the United States and other minority groups who have achieved some degree of affluence. Generally speaking, these men draw attention to their new affluence by wearing flashy colors in extreme styles. Although this look is not suited to corporate life, it does indicate that there is some truth in the observation that clothes and self-esteem go hand-in-hand.

The other group of image-conscious men, and one for whom I have great admiration, are those who stand 5'5" and under. Small men are almost always faultlessly but conservatively dressed, perhaps because of some innate drive to make the most

Short men usually project an almost regal presence. Napoleon was 5'2".
New York Public Library Picture Collection

of what they have. Also, men who are short in stature usually carry themselves with head erect and shoulders back, and they often project an almost regal presence.

The Brooks Brothers customer generally feels comfortable, because the clothes he wears are, in effect, also a uniform. Other things being equal, the Brooks uniform means social acceptance. Frankly, the button-down image strikes me as a case of arrested development. Why should an over-achiever look the same from prep school through board chairmanship to the grave? He has developed, achieved, matured and it should be reflected in the image he projects.

2

Why Even a King Must Care

THE following paragraph is excerpted from a letter that Great Britain's Queen Mother Mary felt obliged to write to her son, His Royal Highness, Edward, Prince of Wales, on the subject of appropriate attire:

> Dress gives one the outward sign from which people in general can, and often do, judge the inward state of mind and feelings of a person; for this they can see while the other they cannot see. On that account, clothes are of particular importance, particularly to persons of high rank.

And yet, some successful and world-famous men care nothing about clothes: Albert Einstein often looked like an unmade bed, for instance, and Woody Allen usually looks like somebody's poor relative. It is difficult to quarrel with success, but I expect you will agree that every man (not only men of high rank) should look as good as he is, even better if possible. If a man is a genius, like Einstein, perhaps genius is all he needs. According to a recent study, however, only one man in 8,600 is a genius. For the rest of us, it's extremely helpful in business or the professions to look the part—that is, to project an image that equals, not negates, one's ability. Unfortunately, most men project an image that must be *overcome*, rather than an image that says at a glance, "You can trust my professionalism."

Woody Allen looking like someone's poor relative.
Woody Allen Productions

On October 7, 1980, I received the following letter from a Donald Silberman in Trumbull, Connecticut. Mr. Silberman had evidently read an article about my activities in the Sunday edition of the Bridgeport *Post*. There were three photographs including one large head and shoulder shot.

Mr. Levitt:
    You are a fine example of the magnanimous person. Your efforts to improve our community are to be highly commended.
    Since you yourself are involved, via your Custom Shirt Shops, with being dressed fashionably, why do you insist upon wearing an eyeglass frame that should not

be seen much less worn? Don't you notice the rivets showing in the front? Stop in at your local opticians and have them dress you in eyewear that will complement your wardrobe.

Sincerely yours,
Donald Silberman

I am a Sales Representative for a very fine fashionable eyewear manufacturer.

It is interesting what people notice. Because of my particular area of interest, I see everything worn by men and women encompassing color coordination, line, and fashion. Mr. Silberman noticed only the rivets showing on the front of my eyeglass frames. In contrast, I've never seen them. It is my hope, and, incidentally, our experience, that the ideas advanced in this book will help you look better without inviting comment on the clothes you wear.

Most men are uncertain about when or why to wear what with what. Later I will propose four simple concepts designed to create certainty out of uncertainty. For now, a few preliminary observations are in order:

1. Most men dislike shopping because they are uncertain about what to buy. Only when choice is eliminated do men tend to look their best, as, for example, when they are dressed in uniforms created by professional designers (military, judicial, and clerical garb, or formal clothes). And don't overlook the teenagers; for example, you've seen how much better they look when dressed in prep-school uniforms. Certainly, a few well-known men have looked as good in business clothes as in uniforms. Two overweight men—Winston Churchill and Edward Arnold—and three skinny men—Adolphe Menjou, Fred Astaire, and the former Prince of Wales—come to mind. But they are the exceptions. If you look better in formal clothes than you do in the clothes you wear to the office, then it stands to reason that the fault probably lies in your clothes, *not* in you. Think about it!

2. "Dressing the part" should be part of the college curriculum. It isn't. It surely should be part of the graduate curriculum. It isn't. Actors in the theater, film, or television are not permitted to

design their own wardrobe. Wardrobes are always created by highly paid professional designers, who make sure that the clothes project an image appropriate to the actor's role.

3. Each year the fashion industry deliberately creates new styles to make the clothes in your closet look obsolete. Even though new fashions make a complicated procedure more complicated than necessary, a man is obliged to coordinate his personal "business uniform" every morning. The uniform consists of five to eight separate pieces—shoes, socks, suit, shirt, and tie (in colder climates, add hat, outercoat, and gloves)—each of which must be bought individually and then consistently coordinated into a whole that should project an image of substance.

4. Of the two million men measured at the Custom Shop, 99 percent were found to be wearing collars that were *three quarters of an inch* too tight—and they *didn't know it*.

5. Eighty-five percent of all men don't know the various ways to tie a knot that will complement the collar styles they wear and the width and quality of the tie silk itself (see Chapter 13).

6. Every man looks better in some colors than others (see Chapter 10).

7. In today's society, hairstyling is a problem and facial hair—the mistakes are legion here—presents even more difficulty. A "freaky" or artificial look diminishes stature (see Chapter 20).

8. Other chapters will

   (A) Explain four simple concepts that make it possible to coordinate an entire wardrobe without effort

   (B) Identify an executive's image choices—at the office and away from the office

   (C) Suggest a long-range wardrobe plan to cover all occasions —business, weekends, and dress-up

   (D) Offer guidance on shopping—where, when, and how to make the best buys

   (E) Explain how to get proper alterations when buying clothes

   (F) Suggest suitable accessories

   (G) Suggest several grooming guidelines

   (H) Offer a catch-all group of suggestions for the best way to conduct oneself in miscellaneous business situations

*Men look their best in uniforms
designed by designers to make
men look their best.*

*And men look their very best in formal
clothes.*

3

Man's Excuses for Not Trying to Project a Better Image

MEN naturally resist doing anything about their clothes, even to the extent of refusing, as *New Yorker* writer Brendan Gill did, to look a clothes horse in the mouth. The real reasons for the American male's reluctance to confront the issue of his personal appearance are usually camouflaged in the form of the excuses listed below.

"I Hate to Go Shopping"

Most men put off shopping as long as possible and then find further excuses for putting it off yet again. If women enjoy shopping—and most women do—why don't men?

One day at lunch, Jack Kling, the director of marketing for a multimillion-dollar packaged-foods corporation, supplied an answer to this vexing question. My wife, trying a little independent research, had asked Jack point-blank how often he went shopping. "Not often," he replied. His wife, Jean, then said, "Come on, let's tell the truth." Jack admitted, "Well, I hate to shop because I don't like to make a mistake. Three hundred and twenty-five dollars for a suit—it better be right. Once a year, I go out with Jean. She prepares a list and we buy everything I need. One shop, one shot."

"I'd like to see some regular-size ties, some shirts with regular size collars, and a pair of pants that fit in a regular sort of way."
Drawing by Ziegler, copyright © 1980, The New Yorker Magazine, Inc.

"Sometimes My Wife Pushes Too Hard"

Real-life melodramas are played out every Saturday in each and every Custom Shop. The wife comes in almost literally dragging her husband by the ear, saying, in effect, "I'm sick of looking at him, do something!" And he is saying, figuratively, "Nag, get off my back. I look just fine." The seeds of divorce are being planted before our very eyes: He can't bear to have his self-image deflated. It usually works out well in the end, however, because, in the end, the improvement is obvious and pleases both.

During the question-and-answer period in our seminars (see Chapter 5), we are frequently asked about the advisability of shopping with one's wife. My feelings are ambivalent. If the wife has participated in a seminar or gone over our concepts with one of our designers, then by all means she should come along. After all, she is the one who will be looking at her husband with a critical eye. On the other hand, as one wise man put it, "A little knowledge is a dangerous thing"—and our experience with wives has not always been, shall we say, gratifying. But usually women understand our concepts quickly and well. The fact that they do so more quickly than men is easy to understand. They are not on the defensive, they are generally more interested in clothing and have been conditioned from an early age to present the best possible appearance.

"I Really Can't Afford to Buy Good Clothes"

Actually, money is not the problem. There is no way an executive can spend "important" money on clothes: that is, "important" in comparison with what he spends on automobiles, vacations, restaurants, medical bills, and taxes. A new Ford costs about $3,000 to maintain in its first year, counting depreciation, insurance, gasoline, and repairs. Clothes that will project an appropriate image for an executive five days a week, fifty weeks a year, cost *considerably* less (perhaps $1,000 annually), yet in the long run they make a stronger image-impact than a new car. As a matter of fact, a poorly dressed executive driving a sleek new car projects an image of instability; one can imagine such a man living above his means.

Make a rough guess at how much more the president of a corporation annually spends on his clothes than does an apprentice salesman. $2,000? $3,000? $6,000? Actually, it's only a bit more than *$400*, as the following table, based on January 1981 figure, shows.

Annual Wardrobe Budget

	CORPORATION PRESIDENT		APPRENTICE SALESMAN		DIFFERENCE
2 suits	2 @ $275	= $ 550.00	2 @ $150	= $300.00	$250.00
5 shirts	5 @ $25	= 125.00	5 @ $15	= 75.00	50.00
5 ties	5 @ $12.50	= 62.50	5 @ $7.50	= 37.50	25.00
2 pairs of shoes	2 @ $65	= 130.00	2 @ $45	= 90.00	40.00
1 outercoat	1 @ $200	= 200.00	1 @ $125	= 125.00	75.00
		$1,067.50		$627.50	$440.00

You are obliged to spend the $627.50 no matter what, so we are really talking about an extra $400–$500 a year. Compare that to the amount you spend annually on vacations, restaurants, liquor, and on clothes for your wife and children.

I think it may have been Gracie Allen who said: "People are funny about money."

One night, after work, I found myself going home on the Madison Avenue bus (my chauffeur was ill). I was greeted by a friend and, as luck would have it, we were able to sit next to each other. I said, "John, we hope you and Joanna will be dining with us soon." John said, "I'm giving a surprise party for Joanna—and your invitation is already in the mail." It turned out to be a black-tie dinner dance, in celebration of Joanna's fortieth birthday. John had four hundred and eighty guests filling the Starlight Roof of the Waldorf-Astoria. A gourmet dinner, the Waldorf's best, was served, complete with white wine, red wine and champagne, vintage superior and a 22-piece Lester Lanin orchestra led by the maestro himself. It was a gala affair and as lovely a present as any man could give to a wife.

The point is, there we were, big shots, both of us, riding the Madison Avenue bus with John wearing his ready-made shirt and looking it.

"I Couldn't Care Less What I Look Like"

This is a coverup. The truth is that most men do care, and care deeply, what they look like and what other people think of their appearance. Otherwise, such matters as graying or disappearing hair, facial wrinkles, and increasing girth would not be the subjects of daily and almost obsessive contemplation, and men would not be going to "stylists" instead of barbers and using blow dryers instead of Turkish towels after a shower.

Visitors getting off the elevator at the executive offices of The Custom Shop find our receptionist directly in front of them. Immediately behind her is a huge floor-to-ceiling mirror. One day the receptionist noticed—and now the rest of us notice, too—that every man stepping out of the elevator looks at himself before he looks at her, even though she is directly in front of him. Frequently he will be talking with her while straightening his tie or patting his hair.

Men really are conscious of the way they look, and they care very much. Yet, why is the subject such a sensitive one? Let's examine the big taboos.

4

The Big Taboo

A CHIEF executive officer (CEO) pulls no punches when it comes to job performance. If it is necessary to call down an executive, he "lays it on the line." Nor is he ever embarrassed to bring up personal subjects that affect performance: alcoholism, marital problems, obvious neurotic behavior, office romance, etc. The confrontation is private but candid.

Yet the subjects of bad breath, body odor, and appropriate attire are totally taboo, even though nothing diminishes a company's image like an executive who fails to project the image established by the company in its advertising, stationery, and corporate-office decor. Thanks to several best-selling books on appropriate atttire, this problem has finally "come out of the closet." But is appearance really that important? Several corporations have thought so, although the steps they took to remedy the problem often seem a bit wrong-headed or half-hearted.

In 1972, IBM's chairman of the board, Thomas Watson, Jr., vented his frustration with tacky-looking executives by issuing a two-page, single-spaced memo that began

> My associates, without exception, have told me that I should never write to you about business attire or personal appearance because my comments would be subject to misinterpretation and run the risk of appearing arbitrary.

Watson went on to say that he had personally confirmed that top executives across the country agreed that a conservative style of dress was still the most appropriate for businessmen. He then requested that each manager take the responsibility to establish and enforce conservative dress and appearance.

To be sure, even though Tom Watson knew something was wrong, he failed to suggest specific remedies (in passing, it's interesting to note that the Queen Mother was so direct in her advice, whereas Watson was so indirect). As vague as his memo was, it was startling enough in 1972 to galvanize IBM executives into quickly adopting a uniform that began with white shirts and later was expanded to include blue shirts and low-key stripes.

Another CEO who spoke up was Ford Bell, the former chief executive of Red Owl Stores and a long-time member of the General Mills board of directors. In a small book called *You're in Charge*, Bell reprinted a series of memoranda that he had written over the years to the man he had chosen as his successor at Red Owl. In one memo, Mr. Bell says that he called in a salesman who was to be promoted to sales manager; he told the young man of his promotion, congratulated him, told him that he thought he had great potential, and then added, "Now let's go downtown and I'll help you buy the kind of clothes a sales manager should learn to wear." Although his goal was laudable, I think that Mr. Bell went too far—one man's personal taste should not be imposed arbitrarily on others. Following our suggestions, a man can easily coordinate his wardrobe within the parameters of his own taste.

An example of an executive not going far enough was supplied by the director of a large government agency, who issued the following memorandum (reproduced here in full):

> I have recently observed employees walking around in stocking feet or barefoot. This is a safety violation which cannot be condoned. Employees are required to wear appropriate footwear at all times while on the job.
>
> Supervisors will be expected to fully enforce this requirement.

The surprising thing about this memo is not that some of the people working for us taxpayers are padding around the halls of bureaucracy without shoes or socks, but that the issue was seen by the supervisor *only* in terms of safety. The supervisor either did not recognize or did not feel free to point out the fact that going around barefooted during business hours is in very poor taste—unless, of course, one happens to be working as a lifeguard.

As these anecdotes illustrate, the problem of appropriate attire is best taken care of by an outside professional, in the same way that outsiders handle the company's advertising, taxes, audits, and legal work.

Of course, the difference between the successful executive and the man who never makes it will be found inside his *brain*, not in the way he knots a necktie. But the executive who projects the *image* of an executive, even before he speaks, feels secure about his appearance and establishes an immediate impression of quality and credibility for himself and for his organization.

You know how good you feel when you buy a new suit, shirt, or tie that you sense is exactly right for you.

Coat Tails

The Big Taboo

You know how good you feel when you buy a new suit, shirt, or tie that you believe is exactly right for you. When you look attractive, you feel attractive, and with a little know-how, you can have that good feeling not just occasionally, but all the time.

5

If You Know How, It's All So Easy

Most executives do not look like executives, and for a good reason —the average man has received little guidance on how to coordinate his clothes since Mom picked out his first pair of long pants. When professional expertise is applied to a man's wardrobe, the results are uniformly excellent. The problem is, there are few places where an executive can receive professional counsel that is not *self-serving*.

Man has received little guidance since Mom picked out his first pair of long pants.

The necessity of helping to help men look better first became evident to me in 1938, when the advice offered in this book began to take shape. It had taken me almost a year to realize that our custom-made shirts, with collars individually designed to complement a customer's particular neck and face, didn't look as good as they should because the customers didn't know how to knot a tie properly, had little understanding of color coordination, and didn't have the shirts laundered properly. Any attempt on my part—and, subsequently, on the part of our ninety-four designers—to educate customers was met with suspicion, indifference, or outright hostility. Many customers thought our advice was a ploy designed to sell neckties. In other cases, customers felt that they had devoted more than enough time to something that from a "macho" point of view was of little consequence.

Business was booming and profits excellent, but I was frustrated. Here I was offering, in effect, $10 bills for $1 and finding few takers. Customers paid for the shirts but turned up their noses at the free "how to service this product" information—an essential, integral part of the product itself. There was no way that I or my designers could break through this invisible wall, until . . .

Five years ago I was blessed with the idea of putting together a slide presentation using photographs of world-famous and successful men, rather than models dressed up to look bad, to illustrate the astonishing lack of competence in the area of dressing oneself. These "bad" examples were easy to find. Good examples were very hard to find. Magazines, newspapers, and annual financial reports were literally filled with photos of important men whose style of dress made the point quite clearly.

The New York Times once ran an amusing story about a million-dollar diamond heist by two men who "looked just like bankers," according to the watchman who had let the bandits into the room that held the diamonds. Unfortunately, executives sometimes look more like gunmen than bankers. The same *Times* carried a photo of Henry Ford in which he really does look like a gunman. Mr. Ford was wearing a loud pin-striped suit, a shirt so undersized that his neck bulged out and his buttons looked strained at the midriff, and a vividly striped tie. Here was a perfect addition

Images can be deceiving—racketeer or "financeer"? (Henry Ford)
New York Times

to our file of "mug shots" showing how a man's attire can diminish the image he projects.

Armed with photos like the one above, we approached large corporations offering to make a slide presentation to their executives without fee, as a public relations effort. Acceptance was immediate, and in 1978 several corporations went even further, retaining The Custom Shop's corporate division as a consultant for selected groups of executives and account representatives. These forward-thinking corporations realized that although we had given their executives valuable guidelines in our slide presentations, the guidelines were not always comprehensive enough to allow the executive to follow through properly; help was needed on a one-to-one basis.

For thirty-seven years I had been a man shouting in the wilderness, my voice not being heard or heeded. Finally, through the slide-presentation and the corporate-consultation programs, I found an audience that would listen.

During the question-and-answer period following my lectures, one question is almost always asked: "Mr. Levitt, you have shown us two dozen world-famous men who obviously don't know or don't care how they look. If they don't, why should I?" I answer with an anecdote told by Woody Allen, about a young woman who was bored with New York and decided to live in Venice. Unfortunately, things got so tough in Venice that she was forced to become a streetwalker; not surprisingly, she drowned. The point is, not everyone can walk on water. And not everyone has the energy, brains, and personality to succeed in spite of a negative appearance.

My approach to the problem of what to wear, and when and why to wear it, is direct and down-to-earth. Among its benefits:

1. It allows you to put together a wardrobe—regardless of current fashion, personal taste, or regional preference—that will help you to always look your best.
2. It eliminates the daily hassle of putting together as many as eight separate pieces by following an executive-uniform approach that gets you dressed quickly and confidently, and without your having to think about it.
3. It provides you with a variety of looks so that you always look fresh, up-to-date, and correct for your particular professional situation—and again, without having to work at it.
4. It provides you with different looks for the whole range of life's important occasions, both in and out of business. You will look "well-born and well-bred" all the time, not only from nine to five.

Are you apprehensive about the idea of an executive uniform? "Employees are reduced to walking sandwich boards advertising their status," declares the author of a recent how-to-dress book, as he somewhat sophomorically takes issue with what he terms "dress codes . . . devised by small minds in big rooms." The actual truth of the matter is that our guidelines provide more freedom and greater flexibility than most men now enjoy. The space for individual preferences that one may opt for within the framework of our approach is considerably larger than the "big room" in which the aforementioned "small mind" operates.

I once provided a mathematician friend with the range of options available if a man has a wardrobe containing five suits, one blazer, one sport coat, twenty shirts, and thirty neckties. He calculated the number of possible free choices as 4,200. I hope this arithmetic makes it clear that you are very much your own man when it comes to assembling your executive uniform. And that, of course, is exactly as it should be.

In the next chapter I will suggest reasons for not taking fashion too seriously—except, that is, for that occasional item that really does turn you on.

6

"Fashion Is Spinach and I Say to Hell with It"

THIS line isn't mine, but I wish it were. Actually, it is based on an E. B. White caption, and adapted for the title of a best-seller written by Elizabeth Hawes, an American dress designer of the 1940s. The confusion that exists with both men and women about appropriate clothes results from manufacturers who each season, in concert with designers, create new fashions calculated to make last season's clothes obsolete. Here are several examples:

1. Dunhill Tailors, one of New York's most prestigious custom tailors, took the standard Ivy League lapel and increased its width gradually from three inches to 4½ inches. The wide lapel became standard. Early in 1979, French and Italian designers arbitrarily reduced the lapel width to 2½ inches. This means suits you bought in the last few years will *suddenly* look old (and to some eyes worn out) long before they actually are old.
2. Neckties rose from a two-inch width in 1941 to a width of five inches in 1976. They arbitrarily went back to three inches in 1979. As of this writing, European designers are showing a two-inch tie for their spring 1981 line.
3. In 1972 Pierre Cardin brought out a new line of shirts with four-inch collar points, thus producing a collar that might be becoming on a six-footer weighing 275 pounds (in other words, a big, "fattish" man) but is totally unsuited to young men and to men with slender faces. Nevertheless, the male animal, with sheeplike docility, stopped wearing old shirts and proceeded to buy the new

1978—Wide lapels (LEFT)
1980—Skinny lapels (RIGHT)
Fashion is an industry rip-off. Forget it!

long-point collars. Now, some years later, designers are showing shirts with a 2½-inch collar, and once again the male animal is falling into line. Only this time, thankfully, there are signs of a modest rebellion.

4. The Nehru jacket, a best seller for two seasons, is finished. It was followed by the leisure suit—also finished. The newest fashion is the unstructured jacket, which looks like and is almost as limp as the gray-cotton jacket butlers wear for dusting and cleaning silver. It's certain to have a quick death.

5. In the fall of 1979, designers in Italy and France began showing fashions that are no fashions at all and that created a look more suited to an alcoholic than a career-minded businessman. It is not the new look that I question; I object only to the fact that the look is so unbecoming.

Fashion has taken us from the sublime to the ridiculous in the same way that some high priests in the art world give the random

30

The leisure suit and the Nehru jacket. Both were "new looks" in their day, and both were subsequently closed out at Alexander's. Fashion is an industry rip-off. Forget it!

drippings of a Jackson Pollock a value equal to the unquestioned genius of a Rembrandt.

Now there is little doubt that fashion *per se* is of more than passing interest to most men, and of great interest to most women. Fashion as an industry certainly has its good side. How dull it is in China, where everybody seems to dress like everybody else. However, the fashion industry and its press have become too aggressive in relentlessly insisting on creating new fashions, no matter how wild, to make obsolete the clothes you own. The following letter, written to John Sias, publisher of the fashion trade paper *The Daily News Record*, makes my feelings unmistakably clear—and if there should be any doubt, illustrations above and facing and on the page following provide perfect examples of what I mean.

It may seem ungracious of me to take exception to books that have been helpful in spotlighting the problem of appropriate attire. But (without mentioning any names) there is much advice offered to which I would take exception.

Typical of "fashion flashes" in 1979 and 1980 from the Daily News Record. *Fashion is an industry rip-off. Forget it!*
Cover photo, Daily News Record, 4/28/80 ("New Look —Perry Ellis Designer")

"Give Yourself a Treat and Wear $25 Neckties"

The author of the above quote may have taken his cue from an old Clark Gable film about Madison Avenue. Early in the film there is a scene in which Gable, playing an ad man badly in need of work, does spend his last $25 on a silk tie to wear to a job interview.

The isolated purchase of an expensive necktie, or any other item of apparel, is not likely to result in a "treat" for your personal appearance if you do not have other clothes that look good with

"Fashion Is Spinach and I Say to Hell with It"

*It's easy to poke fun at the experts—not so easy to project
an image that makes you look as good as you are.*
Drawing by Lorenz, copyright © 1980, The New Yorker Magazine, Inc.

that item. A $25 tie, improperly coordinated, will look like an
$8.50 necktie. Conversely, an $8.50 tie properly coordinated and
properly knotted will look like an expensive necktie.

"White Is the Most Acceptable Color for the Business Shirt"

Although there is nothing wrong with white shirts, this is
really negative advice, because it fails to recognize a basic truth
related to how the naked eye perceives us when we're in a white
shirt. More about this in Chapter 12.

33

The Custom Shop
Shirtmakers
— Est. 1937 —

Office of the President
FRANKLIN, N.J. 07416

When writing to this office, please be
sure to state which shop serves you.

November 21, 1979

Dear John:

I have been a subscriber to the Daily News Record since I started this business some 42 years ago. As you know, only too well, it is indeed an excellent trade paper. Unfortunately, your editorial position on the new fashions is disappointing. The new look (sic) might improve the image of a delinquent or an alcoholic, but certainly not the customers of your subscribers. My complaint is not that you report the new styles, but that you encourage this dreadful look by featuring it day after day on your front page. In effect, you take a position "for" because you take no editorial position "against."

Here is a partial list of retail clothiers who closed shop in recent years: Finchley, Rogers Peet, B & B Lorry, Whitehouse & Hardy, Roger Kent, Kolmer Marcus, Frank Brothers, John David, Webber & Heilbroner and Broad Street. The list fails to include the manufacturers who have gone broke or who are now in Chapter XI.

Although fashion is a way of increasing sales by creating obsolescence, it can, when carried to an extreme, create a money-losing backlash.

I am neither a manufacturer nor a retailer of men's clothes, and fortunately am not affected. However, I am deeply incensed by the irresponsible way in which the Daily News Record,

Herbert Blueweiss and Clara Hancox have abused their journalistic powers, only for the purpose of increasing circulation; and, unfortunately, at the expense of the very industry that supports it.

Feeling the way I do, I can no longer, in good conscience, renew our subscription. It is only because of the restraint placed upon me by my wise wife that I am not telling others in our industry to make a similar protest.

Warmest personal regards,

Mortimer Levitt
President

Mr. John Sias, Pres.
Fairchild Publications
7 East 12th Street
New York, N.Y. 10003

cc: Mr. John Fairchild
     Chairman of the Board

The author protests the Daily News Record's *effort to increase circulation by promoting outrageous styles in the name of fashion.*

"The Dark Brown Suit Is . . . One of the Worst Suits Made and Should Be Avoided"

This advice, like the $25-tie bit of wisdom, is complete nonsense. Brown and beige are very becoming to some men, unbecoming to others. A combination of hair color, eye color, and skin color establishes the colors that are best for you. Brown or beige suits, properly color-coordinated, look good on a large percentage of men.

"Look for Sales—Buy for Fall in the Spring, and Buy for Spring in the Fall"

This is advice that you might follow if you are deeply in debt, in which case you would be obliged to put yourself down by buying close-outs—clothes that have been rejected by consumers for reasons that may not be obvious when your greedy eyes light up at what seems to be a bargain. The best-sellers, the classics, are *never* on sale. Sale merchandise may be tempting, but it is usually worth only what you are paying for it.

"Do It the Hard Way"

The following is a verbatim quote:

Assuming you are mixing three stripes in your outfit . . . if the wider, strong stripes are on the shirt, and the closer, finer stripes are on the jacket . . . then the tie should be diagonally striped with balanced, alternating broad and narrow stripes-on-stripes.

A man following this advice would emerge looking more like a crosswalk on an Escher print than a serious executive. *Simple* advice on coordinating a patterned suit, shirt, *or* tie is given in Chapter 8.

"Sport Coats May be Worn in Less-Formal Selling Occupations"

For less-formal selling occupations, wear a blazer; save your tweed sport jacket for country wear. It makes no sense to have the same look for leisure, weddings, and weekends in the country, when for the same money you can have a different look for each season and for each occasion.

"The Darker the Suit, the More Authority It Transmits"

There is nothing wrong with dark-colored suits, except that worn with a white shirt a man is appropriately dressed for a wedding. Worn with a pale striped shirt, the dark suit is appropriate

35

for business. If a man dresses the same way for a wedding and for business, then he is stuck with only *one* look. It is *not* good business to always look *obviously* dressed up, just as it is not good business to look—for want of a better word—*dressed down*.

In most situations, a medium-shade, unpatterned tweed suit projects a more trustworthy image than a dark-colored pin-striped suit. In one instance, you'll see the man, in the other you'll see the suit. The pin-striped suit, like the bow tie, may project a *caveat emptor* image—"let the buyer beware."

As I hope to make clear shortly, the man who projects the image of an executive is a man who dresses so that people see him, not what he is wearing. Perhaps the following anecdote will illustrate what I mean.

Weekday mornings for almost 30 years I have been driven down Fifth Avenue past the Plaza Hotel. One morning, as we stopped for a red light, my chauffeur pointed out the scaffolding around the bronze equestrian statue that complements the large marble fountain and asked, "Mr. Levitt, is that a new statue or has it always been there?" "No, Fernando," I replied, "I think it's new."

When I got to the office I asked my secretary to check it out: The statue has been there not for 30 years, but for 60 years. Fernando noticed it only because it was being cleaned.

If I were a sculptor instead of a shirtmaker, I would *really* have seen that statue. As it is, all I knew was that the square in front of the Plaza Hotel was beautiful even though I was not aware of the statue. The same can be said for a well-fitting shirt collar, a well-tied tie, and a well-coordinated outfit. One sees only the effect, not the cause.

By now you may be saying, "Just who is this Mortimer Levitt, anyway, and what makes him a better authority than the fashion experts?" Before going any further, perhaps I should explain how I earned my credentials as a designer and an advisor to men on the subject of projecting an image appropriate to one's chosen career. This involves a rags-to-riches story having nothing to do with the "how-to" part of the book, which resumes again in Chapter 8.

7

Mr. Mermelstein and My Skinny Neck

I DO have a skinny neck. Although this bit of anatomical news might not strike the reader as earth-shattering, it was, in fact, a skinny neck that indirectly launched my career as a shirtmaker: When I bought the proper collar size, the shirt would be too small in the chest and shoulders; but when I bought a shirt that fit my chest and shoulders properly, it would be too big in the neck and too big in the waist.

The Custom Shop became a reality because I had this fit problem *and* because I loved clothes. As a young man, not knowing any better, I sported a cane and wore spats and white neckties. When I was eighteen, I even got involved in a "something for nothing" scheme, basically a chain-letter concept, that entitled me to have a suit custom-made—and ever since, all my suits have been custom-made.

I still had the neck problem, however. Then, in 1934 I came across Mermelstein, a refugee from Czarist Russia who had a tiny business making shirts, pajamas, and blouses from his customers' own material. He charged $1.25 to make a shirt, which was produced at a small loft in New York City's Lower East Side. Mermelstein employed seven sewing-machine operators; he himself did the cutting, and his son did the selling by making the rounds of the various cotton-goods houses on Worth Street. At the time that's where I worked, as a salesman for Everfast Wash Fabrics.

Worth Street was then the center for the converters, whose business it was to convert greige goods, or raw fabric, into finished fabrics. The converters' salesmen sold to manufacturers of dresses, shirts, ladies sportswear, children's dresses, and so on. Most customers bought sample cuttings before placing large orders, and those sample cuttings frequently found their way into the hands of employees in the sample room. That bit of chicanery, commonplace of the trade in those days, was the basis for Mermelstein's clientele.

One day I did some figuring. First of all, if Mermelstein charged $1.25, his total cost (labor, rent, overhead, etc.) must be only 75¢. Secondly, it took three yards to make a shirt, and in those days the mill price for domestic shirting was 18¢ a yard. It seemed to me that I could make a shirt for about $1.25 (48¢ for material and 75¢ for labor and overhead) and retail it at $2.00. Since the shirts would be custom-made, there would be little inventory risk. A fabulous idea. In 1937 custom-made shirts cost $6 for domestic cotton and up to $25 for Egyptian cotton woven in England. The idea of selling custom-made shirts at less than *half* the price of the "upstairs" shirtmakers seemed too good to be true, and the more I thought about it, the more I liked it. Even though I was not a pattern maker and had never worked in a retail store or a shirt factory, I knew instinctively that I could do a better job than this Lower East Side "mechanic." I really couldn't think of Mermelstein as a shirtmaker. Paraphrasing the title of an old song, "He made me what I am today—I hope he's satisfied."

My strategy gradually unfolded as follows:

1. Shirtmakers bought shirtings from jobbers—middlemen who would sell cuts of fifteen or thirty yards of fabric, depending on the shirtmaker's needs. I took a calculated risk and went directly to the fabric mill and placed orders for full pieces. The mills didn't want to sell to me. They wanted me to buy from their customers, the jobbers. I explained that although I was opening only one store and one factory, it was my intention eventually to open thirty-five stores. If the basic idea was sound, then there would be a need for a Custom Shop in every major city, and a city such as New York could support ten Custom Shops. The mills finally agreed to sell me

shirtings at a factory-level price, so I was able to effect an immediate savings of 30–40 percent on the fabric cost.

2. I decided to require a minimum order of three shirts instead of the customary one shirt. This would lower costs substantially and immediately increase the start-up volume.

3. My business would be strictly cash and carry—no credit losses.

4. I would open a chain of stores to lower my stitching costs, because my production system demanded at least two thousand shirts a week (I'll explain why later).

5. I would use only a tiny space for a store—meaning low rent and a prime location on the street—because I had no inventory. All other shirtmakers were upstairs, because they had their sewing room on the premises.

6. I would operate in large measure with my customers' money— I would cut nothing without a substantial deposit.

7. I would open my own factory rather than look for a contractor. This way I could save the contractor's profit and pass the savings on to my customers. There was no doubt in my mind that I would copy Mermelstein's process and improve on it, even though I had no idea at that time what his system was or exactly how I would do it better.

I was so sure my new business would be successful, and so fearful that my "fabulous idea" would be copied, that I actually kept it a secret from the real estate agent who rented me my pilot store. I never told the men who applied for the factory foreman's job exactly what I was doing, either. I told each applicant just enough to find out if he could do the job. When I finally decided on my foreman, I took him into my confidence and had him show me how to take measurements for shirts. Since he had less experience in this area than I would have liked, however, it was a case of the blind leading the blind.

I discussed my new idea at great length with the tailor who had been making my suits for many years. He had grave misgivings. He said a retail price of $2 for a custom-made shirt was too low (at that time, factory-made Arrow shirts retailed at $1.85)— that even if the shirts were good, people would not believe they

The author in 1937, age thirty, already wearing his ever-present "pin collar"—a style recommended for most men, regardless of current fashions. Note: *Shirt sleeves too short; no cuff showing.*

could be at that price. He said my minimum price should be $2.50; I compromised and made it $2.15.

I also discussed the idea with my wife and wealthy fathers-in-law (my mother-in-law had remarried, so I got two for the price of one). Despite my enthusiasm, their response was decidedly negative, perhaps because I lacked experience. In any case, they gave me no encouragement at all. This was April 1937. I was thirty and except for a handsome new wife who was well-born and well-bred, I was without stature and seemingly without future. In addition to flunking out of high school, I had been fired from two of the three jobs I had held. Was it possible that my secretly held high opinion of myself was finally to be justified?

At the end of June, despite all the negative advice, I decided to resign and go into business for myself. I went to tell my boss of my decision, but before I could do so, he said that my services would no longer be required. Once again, it appeared, I had followed my old pattern of coming in late, leaving early, and taking care only of large accounts. I was and continue to be a great simplifier, doing everything the easiest possible way. In any case, I had now been fired from three jobs out of three—what a background for starting a new business!

Nevertheless, I went ahead with my plans. In July my stock market securities were worth $10,000—but I needed no cash until August. The August '37 stock market crash reduced my heavily margined account from $10,000 to $1,000. (It was the third time I'd been taken.) I borrowed another $1,000 from a life insurance policy, and with that stake of $2,000 (who would believe it these days?) opened my first store and a small factory fully stocked with nine sewing machines and an inventory of shirt fabrics, collar linings, buttons, boxes, and order forms.

The first store was located at 1370 Broadway, two blocks north of Macy's; in 1937 this was one of the best shopping blocks in the country, in the heart of New York's garment center, where there were plenty of fashion-conscious men. I needed a unique storefront because my store was only seven feet wide and the window space measured a tiny three feet wide by three feet deep. My original storefront (for which I applied for and received a design patent) was made of black Carrara glass, with a red-and-white-striped dome awning calling attention to the tiny window. This awning eventually became my logo and is actually better known than the name The Custom Shop Shirtmakers.

The night prior to the opening, my wife sent me home at

Store No. 4 of The Custom Shop Shirtmakers opened in 1939 at 55 Liberty Street, corner of Nassau. Notice the prices: $2.35, $2.85, and $3.65 for imported silk shirts—custom made!

1:00 A.M., saying I should get some sleep if I was to open the next morning. I didn't sleep very long, but dreamed that my opening was so successful I had to call in police to keep people in line. With this favorable image in mind, I returned to the store at 8:15 A.M. The window trimmer had finished his job. In the window he had placed a hand-lettered sign bearing the first piece of copy I had ever written:

Our Story Is a Simple One

We have devised a method whereby we can afford to cut
shirts to your individual measurements with collar styles
designed to complement your particular neck and face at
$2.15, provided that three or more shirts are ordered.

I thought the copy was splendid; I couldn't believe it came from
me, because until then I had written nothing other than an occasional postcard.

At ten minutes to nine, I had just finished sweeping the floor
when a man knocked on the door. I was stricken with stage
fright. I said, "Sorry, we're not open yet." Two minutes later another man tried to open the door. I realized that if I was actually
going to be in business for myself, I had no choice except to let in
customers, so I put away my broom, turned on the lights, and
opened the door.

After I showed that first customer my fabrics, he selected the
materials he wanted and I measured him. Then he studied the ten
shirts hanging on the wall to display various collar styles, eventually picking out a style he thought would be becoming. I suddenly realized that I had failed to mark the collar styles with
names or pattern numbers; in the space indicated on the order for
collar styles, I had to write, "third collar from the right." (At the
close of business that day I removed the ten shirts from the wall
and took them to the factory along with all my orders. But since I
forgot to keep the samples in sequence, my improvised instructions
became meaningless. What a mess!)

That first order for three shirts totaled $6.45, plus 13¢ sales tax
(at that time, a blessedly low 2 percent). I had decided to cut no
shirt without a 25 percent deposit, so I proceeded to multiply $6.58
by 25 percent. In my confused state this was beyond my ability
(I might still find it difficult). Blushing furiously, I said, "Perhaps
you'd better give me a three-dollar deposit." The customer said,
"Fine," and handed me a $10 bill. I hadn't known that a retailer
starts his day with cash in the cash drawer for making change.
Actually, I had neither a cash drawer nor change. I suggested that
he go to the cigar store in the lobby and get his bill changed. By

then my first customer must surely have had some misgivings, but he came back with the $3 anyway.

Despite this rather faltering start, customers soon swarmed in. They came in off the street, attracted by the window display and by the extraordinarily low price. There were and are a variety of reasons why a man wants to have shirts custom-made:

1. He has my problem—neck size and body size out of sync.
2. He has a favorite collar that is no longer in fashion.
3. He has a favorite fabric that he can't find elsewhere.
4. His arms are too long, or too short, for ready-made shirts.
5. The tail length is too long or too short.
6. He wants a snug fit at the waist.
7. He wants to design his own collar style.
8. He wants the Brooks button-down collar but wants it in broadcloth instead of oxford, or wants it higher (or lower) in the back.
9. He wants French cuffs or a two-button cuff rather than a one-button cuff.
10. One of his arms is longer than the other.
11. He has a paunch and can't button the bottom button of his ready-made shirt.
12. He likes the idea of having shirts custom-made.

I had calculated that the quality of my shirts wouldn't be 100 percent at first, and they weren't; but I knew the fit would be much, much better than a man could get ready-made, and it was. It is not possible to start a new factory and get top quality, but I knew, too, that New York is a big city, and the supply of customers almost endless. As a concept, this turned out to be correct. New customers kept coming, and the shirts did indeed get better. One disastrous day is painfully etched in my memory, however.

I recall vividly—only too vividly—one particular afternoon about three months after I opened. There were six customers, and they filled the store to capacity! Two men were trying to order shirts, and another two were complaining about delivery. (One: "You promised faithfully the shirts would be here by two forty-five; where are they?" The other: "These shirts were promised two weeks ago; where are they?'') A fifth man was saying, "Is this the way you think a custom shirt should fit?" And the sixth customer was pointing out that his shirts fit fine, but he knew he had never ordered a button-down collar. It is said that big trees from little acorns grow—but it would be surprising if anything other than a heart attack could grow out of a start like this. Happily, I persevered.

The fact that I now own 41 stores coast-to-coast, with no partners and no franchises, indicates that my start-up problems obviously were resolved; for this, in no small measure, I have to thank André Seligson.

I had been in business for two months and my head was bloodied but unbowed, when in walked an apparition. He was wearing a bowler hat, black Chesterfield coat with a velvet collar, starched white shirt collar, a handsome black tie with white polka dots, yellow chamois gloves, and a furled umbrella. He was short, dapper, and looked like he could take on the world. He asked, "Are you the proprietor?"

LEVITT: "Yes."

SELIGSON: "It's an interesting idea you have here. My name is André Seligson; I was in charge of the custom shirt department at Saks Fifth Avenue, and am presently in charge of the custom shirt department at Freems of the Waldorf." [At the time one of New York's best and most expensive clothing stores, located at the Waldorf Astoria on Park Avenue.] "If you would like a partner, I'd be interested, and I know everything there is to know about the custom shirt business."

LEVITT: "That is interesting: I know practically nothing about the custom shirt business, but I don't want a partner."

SELIGSON: "Perhaps we can work something out."

LEVITT: "We can. I intend to open thirty-five stores, and we can form a partnership, but only for store number two; no part of store number one or my factory."

SELIGSON: "That would be okay. Let me work with you for the next two months. I'll work for nothing—let's say twenty-five dollars a week, and if this is as good as it looks, we'll draw up a contract."

LEVITT: "Great."

So Seligson came in. Although I had learned fast, it's fair to say that Seligson took over. At the end of two months he brought in his accountant. Together they told me I was bankrupt. Seligson said my business needed $10,000 in additional capital. He would put up $5,000, I should put up $5,000 and we would then be fifty-fifty partners in the entire business, including my factory and my present store.

LEVITT: "But, André, that wouldn't be equitable."

SELIGSON: "I'll admit your idea is a good one, but you haven't the foggiest idea of what you're doing. You can't possibly continue without my expertise, or without additional capital. If you don't agree, I'll open up in competition; you'll never survive."

My father-in-law said, "Mortimer, you are not a businessman. I'll lend you the $5,000, take Seligson in." I was almost in tears. "It's not equitable," I said, "and I can't do it." Seligson walked out, opining, "You'll rue the day."

His accountant said that the customer's deposit was a liability since it was money I owed until I delivered the shirts. From an accounting point of view he was right; but as a pragmatic neo-phyte, I knew he was wrong. I borrowed no money—not then, not ever—and three years later I opened my ninth store, this one in Philadelphia. I learned then that Seligson was managing a ladies' hosiery shop on Chestnut Street. Of such decisions are men's lives and fortunes made.

Considering my shaky start, it might be reasonable to con-clude that Somebody was in my corner. But I would not want you to deduce from all this that my subsequent success was altogether a miracle, even though it is obvious that I was not only under-financed but also ill-prepared to start this venture. What is most important is that despite my lack of experience, I had several good ideas that were responsible for Custom Shop's success.

From the production angle, the key was to find a way to cut shirts to individual measurements without charging traditional custom prices. It costs a great deal more to cut shirts individually (which we do) than it does to cut stock shirts that are piled several hundred plys high and then cut completely by machine. Once the shirts are individually cut to the measurements taken by the designer, however, the big savings start. I devised a method whereby the shirts could be processed on a conveyor system, thus enabling the kind of savings that Henry Ford effected when he developed his assembly line. I processed the thirty-one separate operations in the sewing of a shirt with a similar assembly-line concept. "Upstairs" shirtmakers use one or two operators to sew the entire shirt, a setup that requires extremely skilled operators—almost impossible to find, then or now. Our operators, on the other hand, develop even more skill at specialized tasks because each of them does only *one* operation. The key to getting quality in this system is having the proper number of inspections as the shirt moves down the line. Inspectors must be absolutely sure that each operation is done precisely.

That our inspection system paid off may be seen in the fact that only 3.4 percent of our shirts are returned because of a fit problem, half of which are due to simple typographical errors in taking down the original order. This in itself seems a minor miracle, taking into account that there are fifteen individual measurements (six on the collar and nine on the body) that must be written down correctly, along with seven-digit fabric numbers, and that most customers start with half a dozen different shirts.

I also developed a unique approach to designing collars, one that had never been used by other shirtmakers. Whereas collar styles were always designed by looking at the collar style from the front, I decided to design a collar by looking first at the *back*, since the height of the collar in back has to conform to the length of the customer's neck.

By now you are well aware of my interest in the subject of appearance, and the belief in my ability to help other men project a more desirable image. I confess to feeling that like Pasteur and

Freud, I am a man with a mission, and the necessary zeal to carry it out.

Perhaps the reason for the success of my business can best be summed up with my quote in *Who's Who in America:* "Success in business is not for the greedy. On the contrary, lasting success is the result of giving more without charging more; and the possibilities are infinite."

This book is written for you, not for me. So let's get to the practical matter before us—what to do about looking the part.

PART TWO

THE SOLUTION

"Two Plains and a Fancy,
and Other Trouble-Free Concepts"

8

The Four Golden Rules

HERE are my four simple concepts for putting together a wardrobe that is appropriate to your career. You are free to ignore these concepts; but I suggest you first try them *exactly as outlined*, before you ignore them. In this chapter we will deal only with the first two rules: (1) Two plains and a fancy; (2) Base color and accent. In Chapter 9 we will discuss Rule 3—the concept of "light/dark" and "dark/light"—and Rule 4, fitting your shirt collar to the "fourth" dimension.

CONCEPT NUMBER ONE: *Wear Two Plains, but Only One Fancy*

For example, wear a fancy shirt, a plain suit, and a plain tie. If you buy a striped (fancy) shirt because you like it, don't fight the pattern in the shirt with *competing* patterns in suit or tie. Actually, two patterns cancel each other out, like ice cream and pickles: pickles taste good, ice cream tastes good, but mix them and they taste pretty bad. So if the shirt is white with a blue stripe, your suit should be plain navy and your tie plain blue. Simple, isn't it? If your tie has a pattern, say, brown with a blue stripe, your suit should be plain brown and your shirt plain blue. If your suit has a pattern, say, gray with a white pinstripe, your shirt could be plain gray and your tie plain red.

Al Hirshfeld's caricatures have been considered by most critics to be the work of a gifted artist. Al is an old friend, and in certain

Oscar de la Renta, famous fashion designer, wearing two plains and a pattern.
Parfums Stern, Inc., 1980. Photograph: Bob Stern

Hirschfeld's caricature shows me wearing two patterns—a striped shirt and a polka-dot tie. Never! Never!

ways we are soul mates. But if Al knew me as well as I knew him, he would never have me wearing a polka dot bow tie with a striped shirt. I never called this to his attention because I believe in poetic license, although in this case, Al "gilded the lily."

Two plains and one fancy not only look better, they are also low-key—a necessary first step toward projecting an image of substance. American men, unlike their European counterparts, frequently wear *three* patterns. If you think one pattern isn't fancy enough, remember that men look their *very* best in formal clothes —no fancies at all, just plain black suit, plain black tie, plain white shirt. If you elect to try this concept, you will find thirty additional combinations below; and it's easy to create thirty more, because the possibilities are infinite.

PLAIN SUIT	PLAIN SHIRT	PATTERNED TIE* (2 COLORS)	(POSSIBLE 3RD COLOR)
Gray flannel	*Gray*	*Gray and red*	*White*
Gray	*Blue*	*Gray and blue*	*Black*
Gray	*Pink*	*Gray and red*	*Solid black knit*
Gray	*Yellow*	*Gray and yellow*	*—*
Gray	*White*	*Gray and white*	*Red*
Brown	*White*	*Brown and white*	*Tan*
Brown	*Tan*	*Brown and tan*	*Green*
Brown	*Yellow*	*Brown and yellow*	*—*
Brown	*Blue*	*Brown and blue*	*—*
Brown	*Cream*	*Brown and cream*	*Red*
Navy	*Blue*	*Navy and blue*	*Red or yellow*
Navy	*White*	*Navy and white*	*Red or yellow*
Navy	*Pink*	*Navy and pink*	*Solid navy*
Navy	*Yellow*	*Navy and yellow*	*—*
Navy	*Gray*	*Navy and gray*	*White*

PLAIN SUIT	PATTERNED SHIRT	PLAIN TIE
Gray	*Gray stripe, check or plaid*	*Black, red, or gray*
Gray	*Blue stripe, check or plaid*	*Black, blue, or gray*
Gray	*Red stripe, check or plaid*	*Black, red, or gray*

* The first two colors are required—they represent the base color and the accent color (see concept number two). The third color is optional. However, three solids is also a desirable combination—solid suit, solid shirt, solid tie.

PLAIN SUIT	PATTERNED SHIRT	PLAIN TIE
Gray	*Yellow stripe, check or plaid*	*Black, yellow, or gray*
Gray	*Multicolored stripe, check or plaid*	*Black or any color in shirt*
Brown	*Tan stripe, check or plaid*	*Brown or tan*
Brown	*Yellow stripe, check or plaid*	*Brown or yellow*
Brown	*Blue stripe, check or plaid*	*Brown or blue*
Brown	*Melon stripe, check or plaid*	*Brown or melon*
Brown	*Multicolored stripe, check or plaid*	*Brown or any color in shirt*
Navy	*Blue stripe, check or plaid*	*Light blue or yellow*
Navy	*Red stripe, check or plaid*	*Red or light blue*
Navy	*Yellow stripe, check or plaid*	*Navy or yellow*
Navy	*Gray stripe, check or plaid*	*Gray or light blue*
Navy	*Multicolored stripe, check or plaid*	*Light blue or any color in shirt*

PATTERNED SUIT	PLAIN SHIRT	PLAIN TIE
Navy with white pinstripe	*White*	*Navy, light blue, or maroon*
Navy with white pinstripe	*Blue*	*Light blue, yellow, or maroon*
Brown with blue overplaid	*Blue*	*Brown or blue*
Brown with blue overplaid	*Tan*	*Tan or blue*
Gray with red pinstripe	*Gray*	*Black, gray, or maroon*
Gray with white pinstripe	*Pink*	*Black, gray, or maroon*
Gray with white pinstripe	*White*	*Black, gray, or maroon*

CONCEPT NUMBER TWO: *Wear a Base Color with an Accent Color*

Your suit is *always* your base color. Your shirt and/or tie provide the accent color. For example: navy suit, yellow shirt, navy and yellow tie; base color navy, accent color yellow. Or: gray suit, blue shirt, gray and blue tie; base color gray, accent color blue. Or: brown suit with a blue overplaid, plain blue shirt, plain brown tie; base color brown, accent color blue.

Remember that men look their very best in evening clothes. Why? For starters, the approach is low-key—three plains. But the concept of base color and accent color is equally important: plain black suit, plain black tie, plain white shirt; base color black, accent color white.

Men look their very best in formal clothes—3 plains, no patterns.
Paul Stuart

When you are well tanned from the summer sun, a darkish color shirt is becoming with a light-colored suit.
Austin Reed

To repeat, your suit is *always* the base color. The base colors for suits are black, gray, navy, brown, tan, and a blue (usually consisting of gray and blue interwoven threads with the blue threads predominant). The base color of a summertime sport jacket might very well be white, light blue, pink, yellow, red, or cream; but sport jackets are suitable only for weekend wear, not for business.

The following chart provides some examples of the suit being used as the base color with the shirt and/or tie providing the accent color. In these cases, there are no patterns at all, as in formal clothes. (The examples listed under concept number one also include combinations using the principle of base color/accent color.)

PLAIN SUIT	PLAIN SHIRT	PLAIN TIE
Gray	*Gray*	*Black, red, or yellow*
Gray	*Blue*	*Black, blue, or gray*
Gray	*Pink*	*Black, wine, or gray*
Gray	*Yellow*	*Black, gold, or gray*
Gray	*White*	*Black, red, or yellow*
Brown	*White*	*Brown, tan, or yellow*
Brown	*Tan*	*Brown, tan, or yellow*
Brown	*Blue*	*Brown or blue*
Brown	*Yellow*	*Brown or yellow*
Brown	*Cream*	*Brown or cream*
Navy	*White*	*Navy, red, or yellow*
Navy	*Blue*	*Red, yellow, or blue*
Navy	*Pink*	*Navy, red, or blue*
Navy	*Yellow*	*Navy, yellow, or blue*
Navy	*Cream*	*Navy, yellow, or blue*

If you follow the first two concepts as outlined, you will be pleasantly surprised at how simple it is to color-coordinate the clothes you own and the clothes you buy. Shopping is easy because you only buy things that color-coordinate with your existing wardrobe. These two simple ideas also guarantee a low-key look, so that neither friends nor colleagues will notice your clothes. They *will* notice that you look better, but won't know why. To others you will seem to be an over-achiever, because you will look like one—in which case, you are apt to feel like one. And now, let's move on to Chapter 9 and our last two Golden Rules.

9

The Four Golden Rules Continued

CONCEPT NUMBER THREE: *Dark and Light, Light and Dark*

WITH the subject of color-coordination simplified by concept number two, we can go on to concept number three: Dark suits look better with lighter shirts and light ties; conversely, light suits look better with darker shirts and ties. For example, wear a navy suit, white shirt, and a navy tie with white polka dots—or even better, a white or silver tie with navy polka dots or navy stripes. Remember: dark suit, light shirt, and light tie.

I would not recommend a blue end-to-end broadcloth with a navy blue suit—the blue is too deep. However, if your other shirts failed to come back from the laundry in time and that is the only one you have, then combine it with the lightest-color tie in your wardrobe—a light blue or a plain yellow tie, preferably. Your blue end-to-end broadcloth will look better with a white blazer, a light blue blazer, a light gray tweed, or a beige tropical. Light suit, darkish shirt.

The contrast of light and dark makes for combinations that have more character, summer, winter, spring, and fall. The following combinations illustrate the suggested use of the dark-light concept, using only base color and accent color. A third color may be added in the necktie (red, yellow, etc.) according to personal taste.

BLACK SUIT

SHIRT COLORS	TIE COLORS	
	GROUND COLOR	PATTERN COLOR
Pale gray broadcloth	*Silver*	*Black*
White broadcloth	*White*	*Black*
Light blue broadcloth	*Blue*	*Black*
Cream broadcloth	*Cream*	*Black*
Yellow broadcloth	*Yellow*	
White with gray stripe	*Silver or yellow solid*	
White with gray check	*Silver or yellow solid*	

NAVY SUIT

White broadcloth	*White*	*Navy or blue*
Light blue broadcloth	*Light blue*	*Navy (yellow accent)*
Cream broadcloth	*Cream*	*Navy (red accent)*
Yellow broadcloth	*Yellow*	*Navy or blue*
White with blue stripe	*Light blue or yellow solid*	
White with blue check	*Light blue or yellow solid*	

BROWN SUIT

White broadcloth	*White*	*Brown or tan*
Light blue broadcloth	*Blue*	*Brown or tan*
Cream broadcloth	*Cream*	*Brown or tan*
Yellow broadcloth	*Yellow*	*Brown or tan*
White with brown stripe	*Tan solid*	
White with brown check	*Tan solid*	

GRAY FLANNEL SUIT

Blue end on end	*Black*	*Blue*
Gray end on end	*Black*	*White or red*
Pink end on end	*Black*	*Red*
Yellow broadcloth	*Black*	*Yellow*
Red Bengal Stripe	*Black or red solid*	
Black red tattersal check	*Black or red solid*	

BLUE TROPICAL SUIT

White broadcloth	*Navy*	*White and blue*
Cream broadcloth	*Navy*	*Cream and blue*
Blue end on end	*Navy*	*Blue*
Pink end on end	*Navy*	*Pink and blue*
Blue Bengal stripe	*Blue or yellow solid*	
Navy/blue tattarsal check	*Blue or yellow solid*	

58

TAN FLANNEL SUIT

SHIRT COLORS	TIE COLORS	
	GROUND COLOR	PATTERN COLOR
Cream broadcloth	*Brown*	*Cream and tan*
Tan end on end	*Brown*	*Tan*
Blue end on end	*Brown*	*Blue and tan*
White with tan stripe	*Brown solid*	
White with tan check	*Brown solid*	

CONCEPT NUMBER FOUR: *Fit Your Shirt Collar to the "Fourth" Dimension*

The one article of clothing that will change your appearance more radically than anything else you own is a shirt collar that has been fitted to four dimensions instead of the usual two. The two dimensions usually used are collar size (15, 15½, 16, etc.) and collar style. Contrast those simplistic concepts with the following four dimensions.

1. *Collar back height.* The length of your neck determines precisely how high your collar should be in the *back*. Shirtmakers cut all collar styles in *five* different back heights. Depending on the length of your neck, collar back height will range from 1⅜ inches to 2¼ inches. If the shirt collar is cut to the proper back-height, a man with a long neck will appear to have a normal neck, as will a man with a short neck. To get an idea of what a dramatic difference in a man's appearance this can make, compare these before-and-after pictures of Great Britain's Prince Charles:

Prince Charles, long neck.

Prince Charles, neck looks normal. Collar height makes the difference.

Sir John Gielgud wearing collar higher in back, but still too low in front.

Wilfrid Hyde-White, famous British actor, looks younger because of his higher collar.

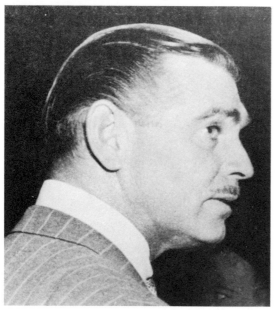

Clark Gable was an early customer who fully appreciated the value of high back collars.

Alger Hiss's obvious long neck made more obvious because his collar is too low.
L. Arnold Weissberger's *Famous Faces*

Richard Chamberlain, the actor,
wears the collar height that Alger Hiss
should be wearing.
Famous Faces

President Johnson looks ten years older than he is because his wrinkled neck is showing.

On this cover, President Johnson's wrinkles have been covered.

A wrinkled neck does create an over-the-hill image. Nevertheless, these three Americans did make it to the very top: presidents Carter and Reagan, and John de Butts, chairman of AT&T. But the wrinkles do look better covered.

It is obvious that the longer the neck, the higher the collar in back. No friend will ever remark on the back height of your shirt collar. He or she will see only that you look better—and, surprise, surprise, you will.

2. *Collar front height*. Whereas collar back height depends on the length of your neck, collar front height depends on your age and the *angle* at which the neck sits on the body. When a man has turned forty and his neck is beginning to wrinkle, the collar band must be cut higher in *front* to cover those wrinkles. Wrinkles are not only an age giveaway; unfortunately, they also create an "over the hill" image. Who needs that?

A man with a military bearing walks with his chin up and head high. Other men carry their heads forward. All this affects the front height and is taken into consideration when collars are individually designed.

A higher front band calls for a larger knot to fill up the additional space. That is one way to treat the problem. A pin collar is the second way to treat the problem, and the one that I would recommend. The collar is made with eyelets, and a gold safety pin keeps the knot in place and creates a military—shall we say, "vigorous"—look similar to the military collar worn by Prince Charles (see illustration).

The fact that Carter, Johnson, Reagan and de Butts made it to the very top with wrinkled necks says a great deal for the brains and motivation of these distinguished Americans. They made it to the top despite the wrinkles, not because of the wrinkles. The average executive is blessed with an above-average IQ. And usually he is smart enough to take every educational advantage available. The number of college graduates—and MBA's is growing. American Management Association seminars and seminars of similar nature are taking place in major cities from coast to coast. The one subject we cover in these seminars is how to present an image appropriate to one's profession and to one's activities. Evidence of this lack is made abundantly clear by the photographs in this book. Is image important? That is a decision that only you can make.

This brings us to the third dimension: collar size.

3. *Collar size.* Several years ago we selected one thousand first-order customers at random and checked their ready-made size (that is, the size they had been buying) against the collar size we made for them. The orders showed that there was an *average* increase in collar size of three-quarters of an inch. The variation ranged from a quarter-inch to an inch and a half—an increase, for example, from size 15 to size 16½. The occasional customer whose ready-made size was correct invariably had a recent weight loss of twelve to twenty-four pounds because of diet or illness. Every other man needs a quarter-size collar: that is, shirt collars fitted to the quarter-inch, not to the half-inch. A tight collar makes a man look ten to fifteen pounds fatter than he really is. In addi-

Examples of men who wear too-tight collars: LEFT: *William McChesney Martin, former Secretary of Treasury;* RIGHT: *Congressman William Widnall*

tion, a snug-fitting collar wrinkles around the tie and shows a gap above the necktie. Also, the tie usually slides down, exposing the collar band.

This point brings to mind the story about a man who gave up smoking to avoid lung cancer. He felt very much better, except for the fact that he put on eighteen pounds, suffered severe headaches, and actually saw spots before his eyes. He then went to his doctor, who, unhappily, told him he had an inoperable brain condition. The man was terribly upset, but being of a philosophical nature, decided to retire and do some of the things he had always wanted to do, one of them being, strangely enough, having shirts custom-made. He told the shirtmaker he wore a 15½ inch collar and a 33 sleeve. The shirtmaker looked at him and said, "Mr. Jackson, are you kidding? Don't you know if you

The button-down collar—another case of arrested development. Worn here by the former chairman of the board of TWA, Charles Tillinghast. His collar is too tight, too low, too wrinkled.

It is obvious that Irving Shapiro has put on
considerable weight. What is not obvious is that
if Mr. Shapiro's collar were the right size, he would
look twenty-five pounds lighter.

wear a collar that tight, you'll have terrible headaches, and worse, you'll probably be seeing spots before your eyes?"

Two Reasons Why Men Wear Tight Collars

1. Men gain weight.
2. Shirts shrink.

It is common knowledge that man gains weight as he gets older. There is a biological reason for this phenomenon. At age twenty the body burns many more calories than it does at forty; however, as a man get older, he doesn't always eat less. The result is a weight gain. When he buys suits, he finds himself going from a 39 to a 40, then to 41, etc. This is an easy transition, because he tries the suit on. Yet when he buys a shirt, he never tries it on and continues to buy the same size until he is strangled. That is the

Evidence that men wear tight collars can be seen by the open-shirt collar look of three arresting detectives as well as by Robert Redford and Dustin Hoffman playing the Bernstein/Woodward roles in All the President's Men.

first reason most men are wearing tight collars. It is commonplace to see men at work unbuttoning their collar and loosening their necktie. I am illustrating two examples: Robert Redford and Dustin Hoffman portraying reporters in *All the President's Men*, and three detectives each with a loosened collar after making arrests. Why do so many unbutton their collars at the office? The answer is obvious. The average man is wearing his shirt collar three quarters of an inch too tight.

The Second Reason for Tight Collars

Shirting fabrics are all Sanforized and Sanforized stands for controlled shrinkage. The fine print, however, reads "less than 1% residual shrinkage." Beware the word residual—therein lies the catch. Residual shrinkage means shrinkage left after the first washing. The total shrinkage is much more than 1%, it is really about 2½%. Therefore, all shirt manufacturers make an allowance for shrinkage—⅜" in the collar and ⅝" in the sleeves. So, a 15½" collar measures almost 16" when you get it and shrinks to 15½", the size originally bought.

If a collar is too tight, that's bad, but if it's too loose, that's

*Fred Astaire in collar that
is too loose.*

equally bad. Here is the usually dapper Fred Astaire looking like a turtle popping his head out of his shell.

4. Collar styles. The illustration below shows the many variations possible in the styling of a collar.

There is no need to be confused, however, because there are really only four basic collar styles:

This might be a good time to clear up a common misunderstanding about collar styling. For example, a customer will say, "I like the collar that Dean Martin wears" or "That collar that Cary Grant wears, can you make it?" The answer, of course, is yes, because we are custom shirtmakers. But what looks good on Dean Martin or Cary Grant might not look good on the customer unless the back height, front height, and collar points are modified to complement the size and shape of his particular face. Only then would it be possible for the customer to wear a collar style that would look as good on him as it did on Dean Martin.

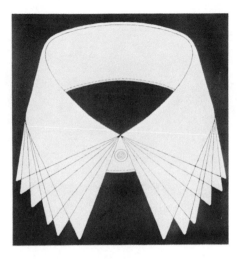

Although this illustrates twenty collar styles there really are only four:
Button down   Regular collar
Pin collar   English spread

The key to the executive look rests squarely on the collar. One must not only take into account the collar heights, style, and size, but also the relationship between those factors and the individual neck and face. In the next chapter, we can begin to put it all together, by thinking of your suit as a frame for shirts and ties that create ever-changing pictures.

*Which man has a properly fitted collar? Only Sadat has a good shirtmaker—
and the difference is obvious.*
Newsweek Cover

Alec Guinness, the English actor,
wearing the traditional spread
collar and traditional classic
stripes.
L. Arnold Weissberger's
Famous Faces

Carter and Koch after they both "got the message" about a collar high
enough to cover neck wrinkles.

71

10

Selecting Suits the Easy Way

*"Quality is never an accident, it is al-
ways the result of intelligent effort . . .
the will to produce a superior thing."*
JOHN RUSKIN

THE cornerstone of good management is planning, and planning is the key to coordinating your wardrobe. Men seldom plan, however, mainly because they dislike shopping. The average man shops sporadically, buying on impulse whatever catches his eye —a shirt, a suit, a tie, a sport jacket—and much too often, he buys the "newest" fashion. Unhappily, the item so purchased seldom relates to an overall wardrobe plan. The result is a potpourri of this and that, miscellaneous pieces that fail to coalesce into an appropriate image.

Think of your suit, shirt, and tie as a single unit, a unit planned so that the three items take on the structure of a single piece. Now think of your suit as a picture frame and your shirt and tie as the picture. In this case, unlike with a work of art, it costs much less to change the picture than to change the picture frame. You spend less and get more because planning gives you much greater variety.

The picture frame (your suit) costs $250 to $350, whereas the picture (your shirt and tie) costs considerably less (for example, a quality shirt at $25, and a respectable tie at $12). You can make fifteen to twenty different pictures for the price of one picture frame, since a shirt and tie form one picture, but the same tie, worn with a *different* shirt, creates an entirely different picture.

If *Time* took your portrait for its cover, readers would see only your face framed by your shirt collar and necktie, the suit acting only as a picture frame. Although this is obvious on a *Time* cover it also holds true in face-to-face conversation.

So when buying suits, think "plain." If you buy a patterned suit—chalk stripe, pinstripe, glen plaid or glen check—you (and your colleagues) will get bored, because a patterned suit looks better with an unpatterned shirt and unpatterned tie. The result is that you look more or less the same—because your patterned suit automatically becomes the picture.

I feel constrained to point out yet again that you may receive no compliments on your clothes; friends will seldom criticize a weak combination or compliment a good combination. However, they do get positive vibrations when you project a positive image. Only a professional would realize that your positive image resulted from a planned, low-key approach to color coordination.

If you own six solid-color suits and twenty-four to thirty shirts and ties in assorted patterns and colors, you can create an endless variety of pictures. Obviously, unpatterned suits offer you the best value.

The natural shoulder suit—
a timeless classic.
Barney's New York

73

The Style of the Suit

Now we come to the question of which style would be the most becoming to you. The ultimate answer, of course, is that beauty lies in the eye of the beholder. Nevertheless, a few simple guidelines may be helpful.

There are really only three basic suit styles:

1. The *natural-shouldered, or unpadded, Ivy League* suit, made popular by Brooks Brothers, has become almost a uniform with bankers and Wall Street executives. It is extremely comfortable to wear. Although this is usually a three-button suit, the top button is never closed.
2. The *American-cut* suit is distinguished by a built-up shoulder and slight waist suppression. It is worn mostly by men who have not been culturally influenced by the Ivy League schools.
3. The *European-cut* suit, made popular by Pierre Cardin, has a padded rope shoulder, high armholes, considerable suppression at the waist, and a marked flare at the bottom of the jacket. The European cut is favored by slender, fashion-conscious younger men (you are apt to see them at the better discos) seeking careers

The traditional American cut—shoulders and modified waist suppression.
Marx Haas

European cut suit

in businesses that call for a less conservative approach, such as advertising, television, show business, and fashion.

Ninety percent of the men's suits sold are single-breasted. However, the double-breasted style is generally quite becoming, particularly in a blazer. The difference between a suit jacket and a blazer lies in the metal buttons. In the double-breasted model, six gold buttons are immediately visible, whereas the single-breasted model shows only two. The gold or brass buttons create a certain "with-it" look, like military dress uniforms. Double-breasted jackets should be unbuttoned when you sit down and buttoned when you stand up. It may be that the need to do this is the reason that double-breasted suits are not more popular.

A man's choice of suit style usually stems from his social and cultural environment. Suit style should also be determined on the basis of career objective, however, and a man on the way up should take his cue, as best he can, from the two or three top-level executives in his company.

Again, a man's presence, not his clothes, should command attention. Low-key, color-coordinated clothes will give a man

*The Ivy League suit—single
and double breasted*
Barney's New York

presence before he opens his mouth. Conversely, a flamboyant suit
or necktie might improperly label a man as "not serious." The
man himself should be aware of his clothes; others will be aware
only of the image he projects.

If I were asked to make a recommendation regarding what
suit style an executive should buy, I would, without hesitation,
recommend the Ivy League suit—not because Brooks has been
selling it since 1853, but because it has become the "uniform" of
the prestigious and influential Ivy League schools, principally
Harvard, Yale, and Princeton.

The natural-shouldered suit is comfortable to wear and a

76

timeless classic. It says, in effect, "I'm a member of The Club; I got my MBA at Harvard."

Suit Detailing

I recommend that you stay away from anything in a suit that smacks of fashion: a belted back, bellows pockets, contrasting stitching, epaulettes, extra-narrow or extra-wide lapels, **extra** anything. Although I can't predict now the many designer disasters to which you will be exposed in the years ahead, I can advise you to ignore them and stick with the classics. You'll look better, you'll get better value, and you'll project the image you should project if you are serious about a career.

The man should be seen—never just his clothes. Shown here are world-famous Vladimir Horowitz (LEFT) and U.S. Congressman Daniel Flood.

The Ivy League suit is my recommendation.
Coat Tails

Stay away from fashion detailing like the Western yoke on the front of this jacket.
Oleg Cassini

Planning a Suit Wardrobe

Let's start with color. All men look good in gray suits, but your best colors depend on your coloring. Men with blue eyes will look good in blue. Men with brown eyes will look good in brown. Men with pink eyes should see an ophthalmologist. In addition to eye color, it is desirable to take into account hair color and skin tone; taken together, they account for the fact that a man will look his best in one color, and his worst in another color. So rather than buying whatever is fashionable, look for clothes in colors and styles (cuts) that flatter you as an individual.

Once you have determined your most becoming suit style, try it on in different colors to determine which color looks best on you. Color testing is the first step we take when handling a consultation customer. We drape suiting fabrics and shirtings around a man's shoulders to determine which colors are the most flattering. Theoretically, a man with brown hair and brown eyes will look his best in brown, but depending on his particular combination of hair and eye color and skin tone (sallow, ruddy, etc.), he will look best in dark brown, medium brown, or tan. The point is that you can't be certain which shades are the most flattering unless you try on the various shades, to see objectively which is the most suitable for you. Your second-best color should be close to the best. But beware of the third color—it could be bad, and increase city pallor instead of counteracting it.

The following guidelines should be helpful:

1. Brown hair with brown eyes is apt to look best in brown and gray.
2. Brown hair with blue eyes is apt to look best in brown and blue.
3. Black hair with blue eyes is apt to look best in blue and gray.
4. Gray hair and blue eyes is apt to look best in gray and blue.
5. Gray hair with brown eyes is apt to look best in gray and brown.
6. Blond hair with brown eyes is apt to look best in brown and gray.
7. Blond hair with blue eyes is apt to look best in brown and blue.

The overall effect must be measured by the combination of suit, shirt and tie—but more about that later.

Suggested Sequence for Buying Business Suits

1. Plain gray flannel
2. Plain brown or navy worsted or hopsacking
3. Plain gray, tan, or blue tweed (buy *two* tweeds, depending on your coloring)
4. Plain navy blazer (suitable only for advertising or fashion)
5. Beige tropical
6. Blue seersucker
7. Pin-striped or glen plaid
8. Patterned tweed sport jacket—country wear only.

Don't make the mistake of buying more than one suit at a time. Look first for a suit that complements your figure. Wear it a few months. If you and your wife are really satisfied, go back and buy a second suit, in the color and fabric you need.

In the long run, it costs no more to own ten suits than it does to own five. Although your capital investment may be larger, suits wear out at the same rate. For example, if you own five suits, they will last five years; if you own ten suits, they will last ten years. But in the latter case, you will project a more substantial image because of the greater variety your ten suits afford.

A Word About Patterned Suits

The Tweed Suit

The unpatterned tweed for business is totally different from the sporty, loosely woven, strongly-patterned tweed sport jacket recommended for country weekends.

There are some areas of the country, mostly in the South (where men are frequently suntanned), that favor green as a base color. Green is no different from any other color, but if it doesn't flatter your particular skin tone, don't buy it. Green is not flattering unless you have a ruddy complexion and sparkling eyes.

The latest word from the Interstoff, the annual fashion and fabric fair in West Germany and the most important men's fashion show in the world, speaks of iridescent (two-tone) colored woolens as the next big fashion happening. My advice in three words: "Never buy iridescents!" It is almost impossible—in any case, very difficult—to color-coordinate an iridescent fabric. Blue/greens are neither blue nor green, navy/reds are neither navy nor red, etc.

The Pin-Striped Suit

Now, what about the pin-striped suit, long a favorite in the executive world?

I give it low priority. First of all, the current popularity of the pin-striped suit makes it a cliché and much too predictable. In my capacity as a head of a philanthropic organization, I recently attended a board meeting wearing my pin-striped suit. When I found myself face-to-face wtih four other board members also wearing their pinstripes, I had the uneasy feeling we looked like cellmates.

The pin-striped suit makes too definite a statement. It says, "I love clothes, look at me" or "See how good I look in my new pin-striped suit." The objective should be to project an image of substance without anyone realizing the part your clothes play in creating that image. The look should be rich but understated.

Finally, the pin-striped (it *is* a pattern), like the glen plaid suit, adds confusion to the problem of color coordination. For example, a gray suit with a white chalk stripe looks best worn with a plain gray or white shirt and a plain black, gray, or maroon necktie—and that's about it! The pinstripe is a definite pattern. That's why you bought it—you liked the pattern. A second pattern in shirt or tie conflicts with and takes away from the pinstripe.

I wear my pinstripe about ten times a year. I also have a glen plaid suit, and I wear it only ten times a year. But I also own about twelve solid-color suits—no pattern at all—and that's what I wear most of the time.

The Selection of Suitings

You will be exposed to a wide choice of acceptable suitings. I would suggest, however, that you stay away from cashmere or woolens that are blended with cashmere, because cashmere wrinklcs badly and wears poorly. Also stay away from silk suits, which usually are sold for summer wear. Unfortunately, they wrinkle badly, don't hold their shape, and are much too warm.

Because the demand for natural fibers has increased sharply, prices of 100 percent cotton and 100 percent virgin wool are actually outpacing inflation. To compensate, mills are blending natural fabrics with polyester. Quality varies according to the price. In lower-priced suitings, a "harsh hand" (the feel of the fabric) makes the poorer quality immediately evident. In higher-priced suitings, it's hard to tell the difference.

Beware of polyester blends with jackets that have "top stitching" on the lapels and/or pockets. Polyester usually causes puckering wherever there is a topstitch.

Twelve to fourteen-ounce suitings (not popular) tailor much better than eight to ten-ounce suitings. They also require less pressing. Tropical weights are usually eight ounces.

Jacket sleeves too long and puckering. Puckering frequently results when polyester is combined with wool. Irving S. Shapiro.

11

Fitting Your Suit: The Picture Frame

AN expensive suit will not be flattering unless it has the right cut for your particular figure and then is altered properly. This chapter provides the basic information you will need to be sure the tailor does whatever is necessary to fit you correctly.

A salesman can verify your suit size by placing a tape measure around your arms and chest while both arms are at your sides and your jacket is off. As a general rule, your jacket size will be seven inches less than your outside arm measurement. If the tape reads 47, the jacket you try on should be a 40; depending on the cut, however, you may need a 39 or a 41. Once you have slipped the jacket on, it is important that the salesman pull the jacket down in front to make sure the collar lies properly on your neck and shoulders. If the jacket feels comfortable, it is ready to be checked for fit.

Most so-called American-model suits have a "six-inch drop"; in other words, if the chest measures 40, the trouser waist will measure 34—a drop of six inches. European-cut suits have a seven-inch drop—if the jacket is 40, the trouser waist would be 33. Portly suits generally have a four-inch drop and the pants are cut fuller below the waistband to accommodate a pot belly.

Some men *must* have all suits specially cut. For example, a man who has a 46 chest, 46 waist, and 48 hips will find that there is not enough fabric to accommodate his waist and hips in a standard cut. The man who has a 44 chest but only a 34 waist will also need specially-cut suits.

Lowering the collar.
Barney's New York

Even though significant alterations are described below, keep in mind that you will not have as much knowledge and experience as your tailor. You do have something equally important, though: a continuing interest in how that garment fits. Some men don't try on clothes after they are altered, instead having the suit sent directly home. If your weight has changed after you have worn the suit for several months, it is unfair to your clothier to bring the suit back and request additional alterations without charge.

Suit Jacket/Blazer

Collar Alterations

There are three types of collar alterations:

1. Lowering the collar
2. Raising the collar
3. Shortening the collar

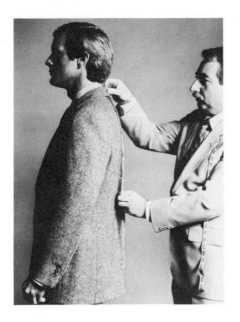

Shortening the collar.
Barney's New York

Raising the shoulder.
Barney's New York

If you are square-shouldered or your shoulders slant forward, you may need your collar lowered. This simply means there is too much fabric across the back of the suit below the collar. The collar is removed and the back of the jacket is shortened, which in effect puts the collar in a lower position on the back of the neck.

If you are round-shouldered, have a thin neck, or hold your head forward, you may need your collar shortened. If the collar stands away from your neck or the lapel stands away from your chest, you also may require this alteration, because the left-to-right size of the collar opening is simply too big for your neck. The collar is removed and the length of the collar is shortened.

If you have a long neck, you need your collar raised in the back.

Waist and Hips

If you carry a wallet, put the wallet in your new jacket or trousers before the tailor marks your clothes for alterations.

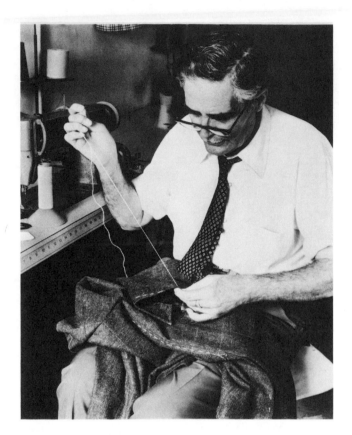

Good alterations are time-consuming and expensive. Barney's in New York is one of a select few that does comprehensive alterations without charge.
Barney's New York

Sleeves

If you want to show shirt cuff, your jacket sleeves should end about 5¼ inches from the tip of your thumb. It is desirable to show cuff, because that adds a finishing touch to your appearance.

Suit Trousers and Slacks

We are now ready to look at the problems attending the lower half of your ensemble: trousers with a suit, slacks with a blazer or sport jacket.

Three leg styles—Continental (LEFT), *Edwardian* (CENTER), *Flare* (RIGHT)

The jacket can usually be altered to fit reasonably well, but in many cases slacks fit badly. A man will look at his jacket in a three-way mirror, but seldom at his slacks. It came as a great surprise to me to learn that women find a man's behind sexually attractive. For this reason (but not for this reason alone, because there are also comfort features to be considered), give proper attention to the way your slacks fit in the rear.

There are actually eight fit problems that *cannot* be resolved with alterations. If you have one of the following problems, you probably are aware of it:

1. Prominent seat
2. Flat seat
3. Prominent calves
4. Bow legs
5. Knock knees

6. One hip higher than the other
7. Low rise or high rise
8. Heavy thighs

Your trousers must be cut individually to correct any of the foregoing problems; they cannot be taken care of with an alteration.

Prominent Seat: Occasionally a man will complain that his trousers "catch" or bind at the knees when he steps forward or raises his legs, as when walking upstairs. This fault indicates that for his particular figure, the ready-made slacks were cut with a too-straight seat seam or were too short in back.

Flat Seat: Although I was unaware of it for a long time, because my suits were always custom-made, I have a flat seat. So with ready-made slacks I suffered "droopy drawers."

Prominent Calves: Prominent calves throw the bottom of the

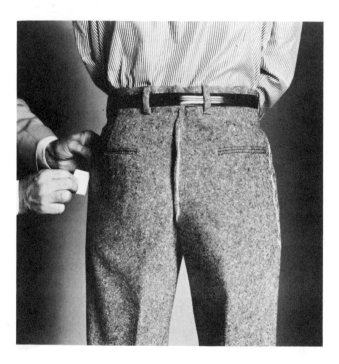

Redoing the hips
Barney's New York

trousers back where they should hang straight down. In any case, the result is that the slack fabric beneath the knees is pushed to the rear.

Bow Legs: The crease in the trousers will not fall to the center of the shoe if you have bow legs; it will always turn out.

Knock Knees: With knock knees, the crease in the trousers will turn in.

One Hip Lower: The problem of having one hip lower than the other is easily recognized because the trousers won't settle correctly over the hip bone. This not only causes discomfort in the crotch, but also wrinkles will appear in the crotch where the hip is higher.

Low Rise or High Rise: If the rise is too high or too low—that is, if a waistline is too high or too low—it is not possible to change

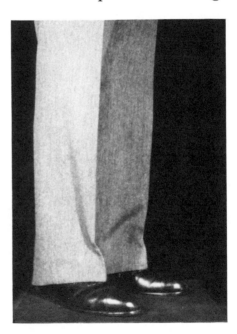

Slacks: Too short   *Slacks: Too long*

it with an alteration. The trousers have to be specially cut.

Heavy Thighs: When trying on trousers, be sure to sit down. If they are tight in the thigh, they'll be uncomfortable, in which case they should be custom-made.

If you are one of the fortunate men who have none of the foregoing problems, I have only three suggestions to make:

1. The most flattering length for your trousers is neither too short nor too long—the trouser should just touch the top of the shoe and should be angled so that it is three-quarters of an inch longer in the back.

2. Unfortunately your slacks, both wool and polyester, will probably shrink after they are dry-cleaned or after you are caught in a rainstorm; they will then look too short. Have them lengthened. In contrast, if your hips and waistline measure the same, your

 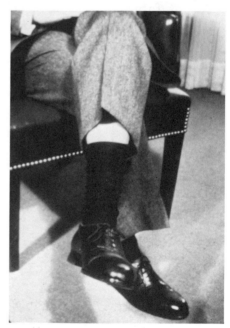

A patch of hairy leg showing between the sock and trouser leg is a real turn-off for all women.

slacks will slide down five minutes after you put them on; in this case they will look too long. To correct this problem, you should wear suspenders. You will look better and feel more comfortable. If suspenders turn you off (and why should they?) settle for the fact that you like droopy pants and have them shortened to the length at which they generally settle.

If you elect to wear suspenders, I think you'll be surprised at how much more comfortable you'll feel and how much better your pants will hang. Buy brown suspenders for your brown suits, gray or maroon for your gray and navy suits. If you have a deep-seated urge to wear fire-engine red or Christmas green, by all means wear them. They'll be seen only when you intend to show them off.

3. Slacks generally wear out long before the suit jacket, and mostly they wear out at the heel. Tell the fitter to add heel stays, an extra piece of fabric at the heel; the heel stay will protect the fabric of the trouser and prevent it from wearing out.

Special-Order Suits and Custom Suits

If you do not have an extreme fit problem, I would recommend ready-made suits.

If you do have a fit problem and feel that you can't afford a custom-made suit (as of September 1981 a custom-made two-piece suit with English woolen costs $850), then you should consider a special-order suit. Brooks Brothers, Saks, and Barneys and certain select other stores throughout the country offer this service; moreover, twice a year they offer a 15–20 percent reduction on their special-order suits. If you think of going this route, you would be well advised to find out when a sale starts, then price the fabrics before and during the sale so that you can see which, if any, are the legitimate markdowns.

If you don't have a particular fit problem yet have ideas of your own about the kind of shoulder, lapel, or shaping you like— and you can afford it—by all means, have your suits custom-made. You will have an unlimited choice of fabrics, you can get two fittings before the suit is finished, and the suit will be designed to your personal taste and idiosyncrasies. Most important, wearing a custom-made suit gives you a very special feeling—and a certain look that does set you apart. Moreover, if it's a solid color and tailored on classic lines, you'll wear it almost forever. A really good tailor will advise you on the cuts most flattering to your particular figure.

As far as Hong Kong suits are concerned, I know only about a dozen men who have had suits custom-made by Hong Kong tailors, so I don't qualify as an expert. But I have never seen a man wearing a Hong Kong custom-made suit that in any way resembled the $850 custom-made suit mentioned above. It's actually a different breed. If you can't afford the $850, then, based upon my experience, I would recommend the special-order suit.

Outercoats

As a general rule, your coat will be the same size as your suit. The coat is automatically cut fuller to accommodate your wearing a suit jacket or blazer underneath it, so if you wear a 40 regular suit, you will probably wear a 40 regular coat.

An outercoat should not be too tight and your coat sleeve should be three-quarters of an inch longer than your suit sleeve.

A Caution

A little knowledge is a dangerous thing. Do not look for major alterations when you buy clothing. If the suit fits you reasonably well and it requires minor alterations to give you a good fit, by all means buy it. If a suit requires a great deal of alteration, it may not be the suit for you. Don't think you are getting something extra because you are getting additional alterations. If the alterations are too extreme, you may throw the entire garment out of line.

If you are happy with the fit of your suit, you can make a friend for life by slipping the fitter a tip—say, $5—when you pick up your garment. He will be happy to give you special attention the next time.

The Quality of a Suit

Here is an excerpt from one of the how-to books that tells what to look for when shopping for a suit.

> First, stay with the classic materials. . . . A poor fabric will not wear well and each time the suit is dry-cleaned it will have a noticeable effect on the material. The poorer material loses shape and develops a tired, bedraggled look. Second, check the lapel edges and other seams to make sure there is no puckering or bubbling. . . . Next, check the lining to see how well it has been set into the jacket. . . . Make sure the lining does not sag below the edge of the jacket, yet does have an expansion pleat. Check the sleeves to see that the lining doesn't extend past the cuff. See that the suit has real horn or bone buttons and that the buttonholes are not ragged.

It seems to me that much of this advice is gratuitous and it would surely be impractical to take the last several pages along when buying a suit. Actually there is really only one feature that does indicate a quality suit and that one feature is, unfortunately, invisible because it is the interlining. Most suits priced under $275 are made with a fused interlining. Fusing requires no handwork and is one of the reasons why many so-called designer suits (Blass, Cardin, et al.) frequently cost less than the non-designer-name, quality suits carried by the better stores. The designer suits simply are not made as well. The quality suit may cost $275 instead of $200, but the make is so much better that you will be repaid many times over. You may not see the difference immediately in the store mirror, but you will certainly notice it after your new suit is broken in. Ask the salesman, "Does this suit have a fused interlining?" You may not get the truth, because frequently the salesman won't know the difference. (In a department store, it is possible that a new buyer may not even know the difference.)

A nonfused handworked canvas interlining makes for a softer half-chest that molds itself to the shape of the body and con-

93

tinues to hold its shape. In contrast, a fused lining creates an artificial-looking half-chest.

Remember that clothes bearing designer names are frequently an insult to the name itself. In many cases the designer has little, if anything, to do with the designing, the manufacturing, or the selection of fabric. In most cases, the manufacturer pays the designer a fee of 7–10 percent of the wholesale selling price for use of the name. This adds between $20 and $40 to the retail price.

Where to Shop

I recommend that you shop only the first or second *largest* clothing stores in your area. You get to choose from a wider selection, and you will get better values. The best manufacturers usually grant an exclusive to one store in a community. The best clothing stores hire the best fitters and are less apt to let you take a suit that does not fit properly. The store usually became the biggest because it originally was the best.

I do not recommend buying suits in most department stores or small clothing stores. Small stores compensate for a small inventory by emphasizing high-fashion clothes, and I advise you to stay away from high "fashion."

Successful clothing stores are often owned by a proprietor who is on the premises, seeing that you get the best possible service. Conversely, department stores are diversified and run by "buyers," salaried people whose positions change periodically. They may spend a few years buying furniture and later move on to the clothing department (or vice versa), that being the way most department stores operate.

Almost all clothing stores run semiannual sales, but only on suits with which they (or the manufacturer) are stuck. Chances are you will not find classics such as gray flannel suits included in the sale: if they are you may be certain there is something wrong with them. Do not buy a suit because it seems like a bargain; it never *really* is. Many stores take an extra markup on an item—for example, charging $300 instead of $250—with the intention of running a sale: "Were $300–Now $250."

On the average, you will save only $200 a year shopping the
discounters. Isn't it worth $200 a year to shop at quality stores
where the merchandise is always up to date? Discounters and
purveyors of fashion do more for themselves than they do for you.
Brooks Brothers

95

In most stores it is customary to PM merchandise with which they are stuck. *PM* stands for "pin money." The salesman gets a flat fee above his regular commission when he sells PM merchandise.

Discounters

The standard markup today for wearing apparel for both men and for women is 50 percent: that is, if it costs $100, it's sold for $200. A discounter saves 4 percent in rent because he has an upstairs location rather than a street-level location; on the other hand, he spends an extra 3 percent on the advertising needed to bring customers to his second-rate location. His other expenses— selling costs, maintenance costs, insurance, overhead, etc.—remain almost the same. In other words, there is no way a retailer can offer customers substantial discounts on new and desirable merchandise. The discounter, therefore, lives on close-outs and seconds. Merchandise that has been rejected by the consumer, for one reason or another, is obviously *not* worth the original asking price.

The discounts offered amount to 20 percent on the average. Since the total cost for your executive wardrobe runs to about $1,000 a year, we are talking about a savings of only $200, if you buy everything on sale or at a discounter. A legitimate sale requires no advertising. Too many merchants run sales year-round. If their sales were legitimate, they would be going out of business because no merchant can afford to sell merchandise regularly at sale prices; he would not get sufficient markup to cover his expenses.

At Custom Shop we have two sales a year, the first immediately after Christmas and the second right after the Fourth of July. Our sale is never advertised and generally lasts only two, sometimes three, weeks because legitimate sale merchandise sells out immediately. We mark down everything that was rejected by our customers. We price it at 50 percent off and replace it with new merchandise. The classics never go on sale, only fashion merchandise.

Does it really pay for a man in your position to save $200 a year on an executive uniform and then spend $3,000 a year to maintain a new Ford that adds exactly nothing to your image? And doesn't the pleasure of shopping in a quality clothing store, with a proprietor you can trust, outweigh the dubious satisfaction of shopping for questionable bargains? It's hard for me to give this advice, because as a result of childhood conditioning (at the age of eighteen I was the sole support of my mother and two younger brothers) I am a bargain-hunter.

I had to laugh when I wrote this because I realized that as soon as it was finished I'd be walking six blocks to the nearest Barnes and Noble, a chain of bookstores that sells current best-sellers at discounts of 20–30 percent. And, on the way, I knew I'd pass a perfectly respectable bookstore that does not discount its books. In other words, "Do as I say, not as I do."

On further reflection, however, it's a poor analogy. The books in both stores are identical, ditto for the credit cards and service. In contrast, the discount clothier carries only merchandise that has already been rejected by the public or merchandise that, for one reason or another, is "IR"—Irregular.

Suiting Lexicon

The following suiting terms may be of some help to you in understanding just what your clothier or tailor is talking about.

BEDFORD CORD: A relatively heavy fabric with a raised cord (similar to corduroy) running lengthwise, originally used for riding britches. Corduroy is made of cotton and is quite stiff, whereas bedford cord is made of wool and is not stiff at all.

CAMEL HAIR: Wool-like underhair of the camel, lustrous and extremely soft. Used either by itself or combined with wool. Natural color ranges from light tan to brownish black. It is classified as wool. A luxurious fabric that looks well and wears well. Used generally in outercoats and sport jackets.

CHEVIOT: A twill similar to blue serge but with slightly round-napped surface. More suitable for business than a smoother, dressier suiting. Originally made of the wool from sheep of the Cheviot Hills, between England and Scotland.

FLANNEL: Plain or twill weave with a slightly napped surface. Perfect for business.

GABARDINE: Firmly woven, clear-finished, warp-faced, fine, close-set diagonal fabric with twill surface and flat back. Usually finished with high sheen and generally worn in the late spring and on cool summer days.

GLEN CHECKS AND PLAIDS: Authentic checks and plaids in true colors of particular Scottish districts, designed in a wide variety of patterns. Authentic district checks and plaids include Prince of Wales, Seaforth, Glen Urquhart, Ing, Dupplin, Scots Guard, Kinlockewe, Mar, Gairloch, Fannich, Locmore, Erchless, Invercauld, Ballindalloch, Glen Moriston, Brooke, Benmore, Coigach, Dacre, Small Glen Urquhart, and many more. Glen Urquhart plaid is the most popular for business suits.

SAXONY: General term for finest-quality woolens made of staple, botany wools of superior felting power. May be stock-dyed, piece-dyed, or yarn-dyed. Sometimes used to designate a particular type of fabric, such as saxony coating and saxony flannel.

HARRIS TWEED: The British Board of Trade and the U.S. Federal Trade Commission recognize Harris tweed as referring only to woolens handwoven on the islands of the Outer Hebrides off the coast of Scotland, including, among others, the islands of Harris and Lewis. There are two types of Harris tweed: fabric woven from hand-spun yarns and fabric woven from machine-spun yarns.

HERRINGBONE: Broken-twill weave giving zigzag effect produced by alternating the direction of the twill, like the skeleton of a herring.

HOPSACKING: An open, plied-yarn, coarse basket weave. Similar to sacking used to bag hops—hence the name.

HOUNDSTOOTH CHECK: Broken twill, four-pointed star check, somewhat reminiscent of a dog's fangs.

MELTON: Overcoating with all-wool warp and weft; the face is napped carefully, raising the nap straight, to show the weave clearly. Made originally in Melton, England.

OVERPLAID: Double plaid in which weave or, more often, color

98

effect is arranged in blocks of the same or different sizes, one over the other.

SEERSUCKER: Lightweight cotton fabric with crinkled stripes made by weaving some warp threads slack, others tight. Woven seersucker is more expensive than chemically achieved plissés that look like seersucker.

SERGE: Twill weave with the diagonal prominent on both sides of the cloth.

SHANTUNG: Plain silk weave originally made in Shantung province of China, on hand looms from wild silk. Characterized by rough, nubbed surface caused by knots and slubs (drawn-out and twisted slivers) in the yarn.

SHARKSKIN: Hard-finished simple twill or basket-weave worsted suiting of one color crossed with white. Nailhead is a larger version of sharkskin. Smooth-finished suitings are better for social occasions, because they are dressier.

SHETLAND: Name should apply only to wool from sheep raised in the Shetland Isles of Scotland. Usually woven with a raised finish and soft hand.

TWEED: Fabric of rough, unfinished appearance, soft and flexible. Usually mixed-color effects. Also plain colors, checks, and plaids. The term *tweed* is now loosely applied to many casual woolens and simulations in cottons, silks, blends, knits, etc.

VICUNA: Wool of the vicuna, a llama-like animal of the Andes, the finest fiber classified as wool. Expensive and scarce. Sale of the fiber is regulated by Peruvian government. Reddish-brown color, pronounced silk luster, exceptionally soft hand. Makes lush, soft, luxury coatings, highest priced in the market. However, it wears badly and is not recommended.

VIRGIN WOOL: Wool is the fleece of sheep. According to the Wool Products Labeling Act of 1939, virgin wool, also called new wool, is "wool that has never been used, or reclaimed from any spun, woven, knitted, felted, manufactured, or used product." The term is no guarantee of quality, because any grade of wool can be called virgin wool.

WHIPCORD: Usually bold warp twill, with about a 63-degree angle and a clear finish that emphasizes the diagonal cord or twill.

Used for riding habits, service uniforms, etc.

WORSTED: Yarn made from the hard "tops" of raw wool. Fabrics made of worsted are closely constructed of smooth, well-twisted yarns. Minimum finishing is required; cloths are left with clear surface. Fancy weaves, stock, and yarn dyes are usual. Generally more expensive than woolens.

REPROCESSED WOOL: Yarn made from wool that has been woven, knitted, or felted into a wool product that without ever having been used has been returned to a fibrous state. For example, cloth cuttings when reduced to a fibrous state become reprocessed wool.

12

Your Shirt and Tie: The Picture

HAVING discussed the picture frame—the suit—let's talk about the picture—the shirt and tie. Variety is a fundamental part of projecting a better image. It is less expensive to create variety by making different shirt-and-tie combinations, much less expensive than, for example, creating variety with suits. To create different pictures, just follow these two concepts:

1. Wear two plains but only one pattern.
2. The picture frame (your suit) is *always* the base color, the shirt and/or tie the accent color.

For daytime, I recommend wearing colored shirts.

1. In daylight, white drains the color from the face, accentuating city pallor, whereas pale shades add color and counteract city pallor.
2. Colored shirts provide opportunities for much richer color combinations; in other words, they enhance the color and the texture of your suit. Remember that a white shirt always looks pretty much the same. Colored shirts and patterned shirts make it possible to change "the picture" more often and more dramatically.

Wear white shirts for dress-up occasions that take place after business hours. Under those circumstances, and when you are fresh from the shower, a white shirt worn with a navy blue suit will be as flattering as a white shirt worn with formal clothes.

For many years, 90 percent of ready-made shirts bought by men were white. Then with the coming of television, white was out because it created a halo effect around the face. Actors were required to wear light blue shirts. As a result of a ripple effect, light blue shirts became very popular. From light blue, it was only a short step to stripes, checks, and other colors. The colored shirt quickly became the "in" shirt.

We mentioned this before, but it bears repetition: You will find that some colors are more becoming than others. Here are several points to keep in mind when buying colored shirts:

1. The color of your eyes
2. The color of your hair
3. Your skin tone

For example:

1. Brown hair with brown eyes: wear tan, yellow, pink, cream
2. Brown hair with blue eyes: wear tan, blue, gray, cream
3. Gray hair with blue eyes: wear gray, blue, cream
4. Gray hair with brown eyes: wear gray, tan, cream
5. Blond hair with green or brown eyes: wear blue, tan, gray, green, cream
6. Blond hair with blue eyes: wear blue, tan, gray, cream
7. Black hair: anything and everything

If you have a sallow skin tone or have brown hair and not much color in your face, stay away from pink shirts, yellow shirts, and bold-striped shirts. In sport shirts stay away from deep colors and bold patterns. Orange and red are always unflattering colors, because they *drain* the color from your face—even more than white.

Appropriate Shirtings

For business I recommend end-to-end broadcloth. It is richer, more distinguished, and usually more flattering than plain broadcloth. Although plain broadcloth is the number-one seller, I also

Handsome suit; handsome shirt; and handsome tie. But the patterns compete with each other.

Now your handsome suit looks better because it stands alone in the spotlight.

Now your handsome shirt looks better because it has no competition.

Now your handsome tie looks its best because there is no distraction. More important, you look your best.

Base color, grey—accent color, blue.

Base color, grey—accent color, pink.

Base color, grey—accent color, yellow.

Base color, grey—accent color red.

An assortment of English fabrics suitable for business, but we recommend solid colors (no pattern at all) for your first six suits.
Chipp

A selection of British fabrics suitable for sport jackets.
Chipp

The classic turtleneck sweater has worldwide acceptance.
Chipp

Heavier crew necks frequently are quite colorful and are available for cooler weather.
Chipp

Wear colored shirts to the office.

Wear white at night. White shirts are dressier.

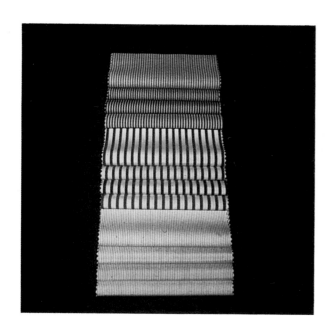

Classic stripes are always in favor by gentlemen. The classic stripe never was out of favor.

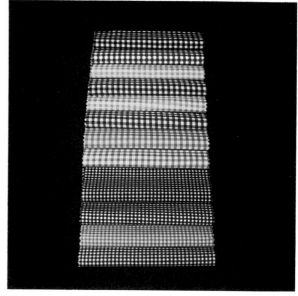

Classic checks are flattering, different, and may be worn for business if not too bold, but they are particularly suited for weekend wear. It is desirable to avoid monotony in the image you project.

recommend bengal stripes, tattersall checks (two-color check: for example, black and red on a white background), monochromatic checks (same check as a tattersall but only one color: for example, blue on a white background). If you buy the bengal stripe this year, buy the bengal stripe in two-tone next year. The year after, buy a variation of the bengal stripe, the classic stripe, because it is less bold; and the year after that, buy a bolder variation, the Regent Street. Each variation is still a classic.

Follow the same procedure with your checks. Go from small to large and back again. Go from one-eighth-inch check to one-quarter-inch check, then to one-eighth-inch gingham check and to one-quarter-inch gingham check—and start all over again. You will always be wearing a variation of the best-selling, most flattering patterns—patterns that have consistently maintained their popularity. Obviously then it will seem that you are always wearing something new and different.

I am not recommending high-style shirtings—satin stripes, bold plaids, widely spaced stripes, etc. New fashions come and go; the classics go on forever.

Oxford is the second most popular shirting and is usually made with the button-down collar. However, we make a great many shirts for men who like oxfords but prefer a regular collar, or in many instances, a round pin collar. Oxford has a totally different feel from broadcloth. It is softer and drapes better, although it does not wear as long. Our customers wear out only four shirts a year on average because custom-made shirts do wear longer. And four shirts a year at almost twenty-five dollars each equals $100. Assuming that oxford's life is only 85 percent of the life of broadcloth it would cost you only an extra fifteen dollars a year, and that's why the "wear factor" is really inconsequential.

I would recommend that you try an oxford shirt if you have never worn one. And I would recommend that every oxford wearer try an end-to-end broadcloth as a change of pace. I do recommend variety, and planning. Variety is easy if one makes a plan.

For warm weather, men who want to be comfortable wear shirts made of imported voile or batiste. Both are extremely comfortable, both are 100 percent cotton, and both are quite expensive —voile being more expensive than batiste. Both come in a small variety of colors, but seldom patterns. Neither fabric wears very well, but man does not live by bread alone, and no matter how much you spend for shirts, it amounts to very little compared with your total budget.

A Wardrobe of Business Shirts

I have been asked many times to lay out the ideal shirt wardrobe, so here it is. I figure on six shirts a week: a minimum of one clean shirt for five business days and one additional shirt for a possible Saturday night dress-up. Since laundry takes a week, what we're really talking about is twelve shirts, and because you would like color-coordinated variety (the shirt you want may be in the laundry), let's add six more. To these eighteen we would add another ten shirts for the high-humidity, high-temperature days of summer. Out of the three summer months in the Northeast, there are about 25 days when the weather is almost unbearable.

THE IDEAL SHIRT WARDROBE
5 end-to-end broadcloth (3 blue, 1 tan, 1 pink)
2 plain broadcloth (2 cream)
1 oxford (blue)
3 bengal stripe (1 blue, 1 tan, 1 gray)
3 monochrome check (1 blue, 1 tan, 1 gray)
1 tattersall multicolor
1 bengal multicolor
1 satin stripe (white)
1 satin check (white)

SUMMER SHIRTS
8 voile/batiste (2 white, 3 blue, 3 cream)
2 gingham minichecks (1 blue, 1 tan)

For special occasions, either business or dress-up, colored shirts with white collars and cuffs add a special touch. However, this may be a little "sharp" for trial lawyers, accountants, and professional men in general, or anyone seeking a loan.

White collars and cuffs look best on shirtings with deeper tones: for example, with the end-to-end broadcloth rather than the plain broadcloth, or the bengal or Regent Street stripe in preference to the classic stripe.

The Button-Down-Collar Uniform

A man with a uniform is generally at ease about his appearance. The Ivy League uniform consists of a natural shoulder suit, worn with an oxford button-down shirt. There are problems, however, with the button-down collar. First, it is not really flattering to most men and usually by lunchtime has dissolved into a crumpled mess. A second problem results from the sheer monotony of the look, along with the cliché effect of top-level executives facing each other in wrinkled, button-down collars. The button-down collar, from prep school to the grave—truly a case of arrested development.

Cotton Shirts Versus Polyester and Polyester Blends

The choice between 100 percent cotton shirts and polyester or cotton/polyester shirts is up to the individual. Each fabric has advantages, each has disadvantages.

A small percentage of men cannot tolerate polyester or polyester blends because polyester makes them feel warm, and men who perspire easily find them uncomfortable because polyester does not absorb perspiration as readily as cotton. Personally, I find 100 percent polyester the ideal shirt. It feels and drapes like silk, but unlike silk, it resists wrinkling, is colorfast, and shrinks more predictably. On the other hand, polyester does pill.

Cotton wrinkles easily, but it absorbs perspiration and, except for oxford or satin, does not pill.

Polyester blends are less expensive, but price need not be the determining factor. Contrary to popular belief and despite the claims of manufacturers, polyester shirts *must* be pressed. If you look in the mirror at your unpressed polyester shirt, you will see puckering wherever there is stitching.

Shopping for Shirts

One how-to-dress book talks about shopping for shirts. The author lists ready-mades, semicustoms, and full customs. In recommending the semicustoms, he says,

> . . . they offer the best shirt available for the money. Unless you have some physical abnormality that makes full custom shirts a necessity, I would suggest semicustoms. . . .

Further on, talking about what he calls the full custom shirt he says,

> . . . fittings are time-consuming, and since everything is done by hand, specifically for you, delivery is rarely fast.

Actually, there is no more handwork on the "full custom" shirt than there is on what he refers to as "semicustom" shirts. In this regard they are identical. If you do have one shoulder lower than the other, or any other physical abnormality, it will be handled by the shirtmaker as a matter of course.

By handwork, he implies that you receive a hand-basted try-on: Not true!

Christian Gagnaire, who is in charge of our workrooms, was formerly in charge of the custom workrooms at Saks Fifth Avenue, a store that made (and charged for) the author's "full custom" shirts. Despite the fact that customers were getting these so-called hand-made fittings, 18 percent of all shirts were brought back for alterations because of fit problems. In contrast, we have only 3.4 percent returned. And much of that is the result of mechanical "typos." We give a fitting *before* we make the shirt, and that is the reason our alteration rate is so low.

Economizing on Shirts

Inexperienced customers bring shirts back to The Custom Shop to have worn-out collars and cuffs replaced. Many customers consider that one of the advantages of having shirts custom-made, but it actually is a poor investment, since the body of the shirt will wear out long before the new collars and cuffs. The fabric will split under the armhole or at the neckline, having been weakened either by perspiration and friction under the arm or by the strain of ripping the worn collar from the shirt at the neckline.

Let's look at the money problem squarely. Our customers wear out *only four shirts a year*, because custom-made shirts do wear much longer than ready-mades. So, if you were to spend $5 a shirt more than you are accustomed to spending, you would be spending an extra $20 a year for the privilege and pleasure of having shirts custom-made to your individual measurements with collars designed to complement your particular neck and face. You cannot save real money by economizing on shirts. You can save important money by economizing on automobiles and vacations in Europe or the Caribbean.

Recently I attended a small party at Gracie Mansion, the temporary home of New York City mayor Ed Koch. One of the guests, upon learning of my identity, immediately introduced himself. Under the circumstances he shall remain nameless, but he is the chairman of the board of a multibillion-dollar conglomerate. He told me, at once, that he has been a Custom Shop customer for twenty years and has always bought his shirts in January and July during our semiannual sale on ready-made shirts and ties. His annual salary in 1979 (including bonus but excluding stock options) was listed in *Business Week* as $742,000. Yet here he was, saving pennies by buying shirts on sale—shirts that had already been rejected by our regular customers!

The ways of a man and his money, like the ways of a man and a maid, defy logic. Take this point, made by another author:

> Let's say you are looking for a blue shirt. Obviously, the very best blue dress shirt can be found in the expensive store—but the same shade of blue can be found at a moderate price, and it can be found at a really cheap price. If you're really strapped for money, you should probably go for the cheapest, as long as it has the appropriate look. It won't fit as well, it won't last as long; it won't feel as good; but under a suit and jacket, and with a decent tie, only an expert could tell.

107

The writer obviously is not a shirtmaker. Agreed, the better shirt has more expensive fabric, and a better-made collar. However, if the collar hasn't been individually fitted to the fourth dimension, you will *not* look better. Remember that the difference between a cheap shirt and an expensive shirt rests mostly with the quality of the fabric. A custom shirt made from inexpensive fabric will look more expensive than a high-priced ready-made shirt, because the collar was individually designed. And although it is true that the body of the shirt is covered by the jacket, it is equally true that the man wearing it knows he is covering up an ill-fitting shirt, in the same sense that (perish the thought) he knows he is wearing underwear and/or socks for a second day. But it is done at the expense of his *inner* security.

Ready-Made Shirts

About eight years ago, collar styling became an important fashion feature, and stores were obliged to carry many different collar styles, thereby creating too large an inventory. They compensated for this by carrying only "average" sleeve lengths. That means a 32-sleeve must settle for a 33, and a 34-sleeve must settle for a 35.

On November 18, 1979, shortly after Senator Edward Kennedy made the announcement that he would seek the presidency, he appeared on national television on *Face the Nation*. I was surprised to see him wearing a ready-made shirt. I knew it was ready-made because:

1. The collar was too tight even though he had lost 18 pounds (he wanted to improve his image during the campaign).
2. His shirt had an "adjustable" cuff.

It amused me to think that Senator Kennedy, who would never wear a suit that hadn't been properly altered, would take this chintzy (or perhaps nonthinking) approach to the one article of outer apparel that is not only the most intimate (it fits next to the skin), but also the most important, because the collar "framed his face" and was highly visible during the entire broadcast. Only a shirtmaker would know that the collar was too tight, but everyone would think he had "gained" weight. More, the *effect* of the tight collar established a "rumpled" image, not a presidential image, despite the fact that his face had been carefully made up by a cosmetician. If a man of his position and wealth, when campaigning for the presidency of the United States on national television, has so little awareness of the poor image resulting from a tight collar, what can be expected of executives on the way up, or even other executives whose brains and energy took them to the top "in spite of" and not "because of"?

Actually, salesmen in the country's best stores do not know how to take a measurement for collar size. As an experiment, I had six of my executives go to several of the better men's stores in New York City and ask to have their collar sizes verified. The results, along with their actual collar sizes, follow.

INDIVIDUAL	STORE VISITED	DATE	STORE'S RECOM- MENDED COLLAR SIZE	ACTUAL COLLAR SIZE
Arthur Reis	*Brooks Brothers*	*10/30/79*	*15½*	*16¼*
Custom Shop manager				
Steve Henriques	*Macy's*	*10/18/79*	*15½*	*16¼*
Custom Shop designer	*Barney's*	*10/18/79*	*16*	*16¼*
Anthony Bergamo	*Saks 5th Avenue*	*10/22/79*	*16½*	*17¼*
Executive vice-president				
Louis Giugliano	*Saks 5th Avenue*	*10/22/79*	*14½*	*15½*
Custom Shop manager				
Jerry McCluskey	*Brooks Brothers*	*10/24/79*	*15*	*16½*
Custom Shop asst. manager				
Larry Engell	*Saks 5th Avenue*	*10/16/79*	*15½*	*16*
Vice-president, training	*Barney's*	*10/17/79*	*15½*	*16*

This modest experiment was undertaken after I had been incorrectly measured by one of the world's leading custom shirtmakers, A. Sulka & Company. At their Los Angeles branch in the prestigious Beverly Wilshire Hotel, they recommended a 14½ collar for me; in their New York store, they recommended a 14¾ collar. My correct size is 15½.

To further complicate matters, the federal government has established standards of collar size in relation to chest size. For example:

14½ collar = 36-inch chest
15   collar = 38-inch chest
15½ collar = 40-inch chest
16   collar = 42-inch chest
16½ collar = 44-inch chest
17   collar = 46-inch chest
17½ collar = 48-inch chest

If any of my executives had bought his correct collar size, the chest and waist dictated by these standards would have been much too big. For comfort reasons, chest fit and waist fit are important, but they are secondary in importance to collar fit. And as I pointed out earlier, 99 percent of all men wear collars that are too tight, by anywhere from one-quarter inch to 1¼ inch. It really is difficult to get a ready-made shirt that makes you look your best—and I *know*. Although our profit on ready-made shirts is the same as on custom-made shirts, it makes me sad to watch ready-mades being bought.

Unfortunately, men who want shirts custom-made usually come in for the wrong reason: They want a good fit in the waist, but ignore the fact that they have a bad fit in the collar, because they don't realize that there is anything wrong with the collar.

The Body-Fitting Army Shirt

World War II, and subsequently the Korean and Vietnam wars, made young men extremely conscious of body fit. As a result of military basic training, they acquired both good figures and good posture. Much of the time they dressed without jackets. So it became customary for the local PX tailor to cut the shirt down through the chest and waist to give the soldier a fit that showed off his handsome body. When he returned to civilian life, he wanted that look for his civilian shirts, forgetting that most of the time in civilian life he wears a jacket that covers the body of the shirt. To compound the error, he ignored the fact that the ever-visible collar was, for one reason or another, unbecoming.

Although the shirt collar is, in my opinion, the single most important part of your wardrobe, it won't work if your necktie is not handled correctly. So let's look at that in our next chapter.

13

"A Well-Tied Tie Is the First Serious Step in Life"—Oscar Wilde

AFTER your shirt collar, your necktie is probably the most misunderstood and most abused article of apparel in your wardrobe. Abused, because based on personal observation, barely two men in a hundred know how to knot a tie properly. There are five basic knot styles: the four-in-hand knot; the double four-in-hand knot; the Windsor knot (made famous by Edward, Prince of Wales); the half-Windsor knot; and finally, the Custom Shop knot created in 1956 by one of our designers (now retired), Eddy Edwards—the knot I recommend.

The one mistake that all men seem to make, regardless of which knot they use, is to pull the knot too tight. This causes the tie to wrinkle excessively and eliminates any vestige of elegance. The beauty of the knot that Eddy Edwards devised is that it permits a man to tie it as tightly as he likes and still keep it soft on top.

Another common mistake is to yank on the knot in seeking anxiously to unbutton too-tight shirt collars. Ties will last longer if, instead of yanking, men would simply reverse the steps of tying the knot. This takes only a moment, but it ensures that a well-made tie will hold its shape for years rather than months.

How wide should your necktie be? If it were up to the tie industry, they would have you throw out your old neckties every two years. They change the width gradually from very narrow to very

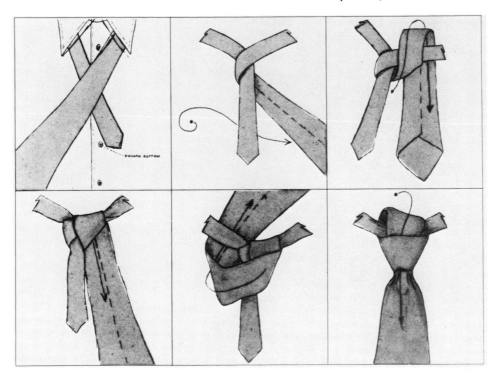

The illustration above is a mirror image; therefore, propping it next to the mirror makes it easier to following the instructions. The manager at any Custom Shop will be pleased to explain the subtleties of tying this knot— at no obligation.

wide. Once it reaches its widest point (5″), they suddenly drop it back to 2″ and start all over again. If you stay with the classic look, about 3½″, your tie will last longer, and you will never look "freaky" or "way out."

The Proper Effect

Certain authorities expect the necktie to compensate for ill-fitting suits, ill-fitting shirts, and unfortunate color combinations. But an ill-fitting collar has attention drawn to it by a necktie, and it makes little sense to expect that a necktie can make a difference

The classic width, always in style—3¼ inches.

1978—the 4½ inch tie

1980—the 2 inch tie

in the way a suit fits. Your necktie is only one-third of the suit/shirt/necktie unit. All three must work *together* to form an attractive picture. If the tie is no more important than the suit or the shirt, then a tie whose pattern or color conflicts with the rest of the "unit" will spoil an otherwise attractive ensemble.

There is a widespread lack of understanding about what tie fabrics are appropriate to wear with what suit fabrics. Almost all men, and most women, buy ties because they are "pretty," "handsome," "stunning," "exciting," "different." The proud possessor of this "fantabulous cravat" then proceeds to knot it incorrectly. When he looks in the mirror, however, he sees *only* his new necktie, with no awareness of the suit, shirt, or the ensemble. A sophisticated buyer may have some awareness of color. But based upon my observation of men on the street, the windows in men's stores, and men's fashion magazines, this expensive, spectacular cravat will usually be one of three patterns all fighting for attention. Hopefully, as a result of this book and of the lectures that we have

114

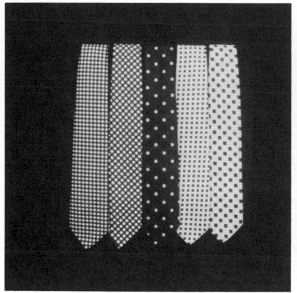

Small patterned foulards and neat stripes—both appropriate for business.
Flashy patterns and jacquarded satins were designed for party wear only.

been giving to executives, the necktie will find its rightful place: namely, if it is patterned, it will be complemented by a plain suit and plain shirt containing the two major colors in the necktie.

As men come more and more to appreciate the understated elegance of formal clothes, they are learning to wear fewer patterns and, frequently, no patterns at all: a plain navy blue suit, plain blue end-to-end broadcloth shirt, and plain yellow knit tie, for example, or a gray flannel suit, gray end-to-end broadcloth shirt, and plain scarlet silk-rep tie; or a brown flannel suit, pink end-to-end broadcloth shirt, and plain brown tie. In the first two cases the necktie is the accent color. In the third case, the shirt is the accent color, but it's the brown tie that makes the pink shirt look so good.

A Note about Price

The necktie is the one item on which both men and women frequently are grossly extravagant, a $15–$25 tie being not considered unusual. Not too long ago, our dinner guests were held spellbound with a description of a $65 necktie found in Las Vegas. Subsequently, *The New York Times* carried a story about a Beverly Hills store that has neckties priced at $160—even crazier. Spending $25 (or even $65) for a necktie carries no guarantee of an improved image.

Basic Tie Wardrobe

Anyone who merchandises neckties will recognize the following categories; however, it is doubtful that the man who sells you the ties will be aware of the differences.

Although there is an infinite variety of necktie designs, there are really only a few basic weaves. The following categories can be worn for any occasion except dress-up:

> *Knit*
> *Grenadine*
> *Rep*
> *Ottoman*
> *Shantung*
> *Printed foulard*
> *Macclesfield*

The following categories can be worn for dress-up occasions only. They are not appropriate for business:

> *Satin*
> *Peau de Soie (a matte-finished satin)*
> *French Natté (a satin basketweave)*
> *Jacquard (satin patterns on a plain ground)*

The weaves you select reflect your personal taste, but don't forget that satins and jacquards are dress-up ties and not really suited for the office. Your tie should be silk if you can afford it; if you can't, the new polyesters make an adequate substitute at half the price.

A basic tie wardrobe requires a large selection of solid-color ties:

> *Navy*
> *Black*
> *Light blue*
> *Beige*
> *Brown*
> *Silver (the palest gray)*
> *Yellow*
> *Maroon*
> *Scarlet*

Color-coordinating a patterned tie is easy: if your shirt is blue, the tie should have blue in it; if the shirt is white, the tie should have white in it; if the shirt is tan, the tie should have tan in it; if the shirt is yellow, the tie should have yellow in it. If the tie has a second color, that color should be the base color of the suit. A tie can have three, four, or even five colors, as long as one can clearly see the base color (from the suit) and the accent color (from the shirt).

So, based upon your wardrobe of suits and shirts, you should have, in addition to nine solid-color neckties, six striped ties, six printed silk foulards, and six small-figure macclesfields (woven patterns).

Bow Ties

Although there seems to be no logical explanation of why this is so, bow ties evoke radically different reactions from different people.

The bow tie probably gets its questionable reputation from the pitchman—the fast-talking barker at fairs, side shows, and circuses or the man found selling articles of dubious quality on the main thoroughfares of major cities. The pitchman, as seen in film, usually works without a jacket. He wears a bowler hat, arm bands to hold up his sleeves, and a bow tie. It might be that image that

The author wearing his ever-present bow tie.

makes a bow-tie-wearing-businessman suspect. In contrast, Winston Churchill never wore anything other than a bow tie, and while he may have been considered by some to be a pitchman, it was always for a worthy cause. And paradoxically, the bow tie is part of a man's most conservative uniform—his formal clothes.

I don't remember when I started to wear bow ties or why. I do know that in my early twenties I wore nothing but knit ties—mostly black, some yellow, and some white piqué ties that I had made specially for my personal use. Somewhere along the line, I must have tried a bow tie and liked it, and I have been wearing them ever since. From time to time I put on a long tie, don't like the way I look in it, and take it off. Being in the fashion business, and not having personal customers, I feel my bow tie is appropriate.

I will say, however, that it does cause frequent comment, and it is for this reason that I would not recommend it to any man who needs to be taken seriously by his client: a CPA, attorney, financial advisor, insurance agent, etc. The bow tie *is* fine for artists, and executives in advertising, public relations, and fashion.

14

Different Strokes for Different Folks: Looking the Part

GENERALLY speaking, businessmen and professional men will look better and feel more comfortable if they dress according to my four concepts. However, what a man wears may vary according to what he does.

Trial Lawyer

A trial lawyer will make a better impression with the jury if he wears a plain gray tweed suit; a blue end-to-end broadcloth or oxford shirt, preferably with a pin collar; and a small patterned or low-key-striped necktie in gray and blue. A patterned suit (pinstripe or glen plaid) will be too loud, a solid navy suit too obviously "dressed up" for the occasion; in either case the jury will see the clothes, not the man.

Bankers and Brokers

Bankers, stockbrokers, and top-level corporate executives would be well advised to follow the suggestions made for lawyers. Although I do not necessarily recommend the style, these men traditionally lean toward the Ivy League–cut suit. For those who dress *only* in white oxford shirts with button-down collars, I suggest they re-read the section on appropriate business shirts.

Bill Blass dressed for "business" in a plain tweed suit and a silk foulard necktie. A look recommended for most business and professional men during working hours.

The importance of the image projected by a banker or stock-broker is illustrated in the following story. In 1958 Estelle Ruben-stein, my financial advisor for the past thirty-nine years, said that some of my funds should be invested in common stocks. I asked a banker friend to recommend someone to handle the investments, and he recommended Armand Erpf, at that time Loeb, Rhoades's "man of the year" and a Wall Street celebrity, and another man—whose name I have forgotten—at Lehman Brothers. I went to Lehman Brothers first, but the man looked so tacky in his "puck-

Bill Blass, after business, dresses up for partying.

ered" 65/35 buttondown that I failed to give him the serious attention he deserved based upon the recommendation I had been given.

In contrast, Armand Erpf—who, incidentally, was both articulate and bright—looked too sharp. His highly polished fingernails, white-on-white custom-made shirt, and black mohair custommade suit projected an image that would have pleased the hostess of an elaborate dinner party but certainly was a bit much for a man who took the business of money seriously. I felt I just couldn't trust him. He was *too* good, *too* smooth.

I relate this incident because, in retrospect, I see quite clearly just how important *image* can be. In both cases it was the *look* that turned me off, and I selected neither man. The man I did choose, Imre de Vegh, founder of the de Vegh Fund, was not only bright and articulate, but the image he projected was just right— not tacky, not sharp, but somewhere in-between.

One night at dinner I recounted this incident and one of the two men present, a real estate tycoon, commented,

> That's funny, because I had a similar incident this week. You know the Sheehans, of course. We were there for dinner last week and I knew that Maria _____ [a well-known television personality] and her husband were going to be there. I looked forward to meeting them both —she for obvious reasons, and he because he was a mortgage broker. I had just decided to start a new division and was looking for a bright, experienced young man to head it up. I took one look at him when we were introduced and never spoke to him again. His appearance turned me off.

It so happens that "Maria" and her husband are very close friends. Actually, he is witty, knowledgeable and a real charmer, with an

Executives in the glamor industries— fashion, advertising, show biz— frequently wear navy blazers with gray flannel trousers, but the red vest should be reserved for parties.
Stanley Blacker

endless source of anecdotes. However, he doesn't *look* as good as he should, and I told him so several times. Like Brendan Gill, he shrugged it off, saying, "Oh, you say that to all the boys."

Engineers, Architects, and Professors

Engineers, architects, college professors, as a generalization, work in less formal situations. For these men, plain tweed suits and plain wool flannels are particularly appropriate.

Art Directors, Advertising, Show Biz

An art director or an executive in advertising, television, motion pictures, music, cosmetics, or fashion will probably create a more suitable image wearing a navy blue blazer with well-pressed gray flannel slacks and Gucci loafers. These men should be projecting a contemporary look, a "with-it" look, a fashion look. They are more apt to wear the newest "designer" styles, the European cuts, etc. Although I am against fashion *per se,* these men (if they can afford it and have the figure for it—tall and lean) should project an image that is quite different from that of a banker or professional man.

Wearing Clothes Appropriate to the Occasion

If you wear your "Sunday best" to an important business meeting on Wednesday, what do you wear to a wedding, a dinner party, a theater benefit, or an extravagant bar mitzvah? On the other hand, if you wear a turtleneck to the office on Friday, what are you going to wear to the football game on Saturday?

Pin-striped suits worn with white collars on colored and/or strongly striped shirts are currently very popular. However, they should be reserved for special occasions—a board meeting, a cocktail party, or the theater.

The importance of a tweed suit in a man's wardrobe is generally underestimated. A plain, tightly woven tweed suit, along with a gray flannel suit, should be the backbone of your business

There is one obvious *difference between party dress-up and
business dress. Save your navy suit and white shirts for going out.
Wear tweeds and flannels with classic striped shirtings to the office.*
Daks

wardrobe. Strongly patterned tweed sport jackets and loosely
woven or coarse tweed suits should be reserved for weekends.
Basically, a man has four occasions for which he should have appropriate clothes, regardless of his profession:

1. Everyday business
2. Special business appointments

125

3. Dress-up social occasions (weddings, theater, dinner parties)
4. Weekends in town or country

It Costs No More

It costs no more to have appropriate clothes on hand for each of the four occasions. Strong-tweed sport jackets are appropriate for weekends. Unpatterned tweed suits, along with gray flannel and brown hopsacking, gabardine, twill, glen plaid, and saxony weaves, are all appropriate for everyday business. The navy blue suit is appropriate for any social occasion. Dressier fabrics (sharkskin, pinhead, unfinished worsted, pinstripe) are appropriate for important business meetings.

The point is not that everybody should dress like everybody else. Tailor my guidelines to complement you individually—your work situation, your coloring, your personal preferences. These variables will affect your choices and give you the individuality necessary to make you feel like the unique personality you really are.

Robert Shaw, the English actor, whose typical tweed hat was much too small for his enormous face. Proportions are essential, regardless of fashion.
L. Arnold Weissberger's *Famous Faces*

126

15

That Old Trench Coat and What To Do with It

OVERCOATS last a long, long time, so it's doubly desirable that they be conservative in fabric, color, and cut. Select a gray coat for when you wear black shoes, and a brown coat for when you wear brown shoes.

Burberry—the ever present trench coat.

Trench Coats

The all-encompassing raincoat owes its popularity to the dashing look of Army officers in their World War II trench coats. Remember Humphrey Bogart and the other macho figures in World War II films?

But the world moves on, and it may be rightly said that the man who wears his trench coats around the clock may also be considered, along with the man who wears his button-down shirt from prep school to the grave, a case of arrested development.

By all means, buy as good a quality raincoat as you can afford. It is indeed very becoming—but save it for rainy days.

The conventional "box coat" with minimum padding in the shoulders is your best bet for style. You will find this model in both single-breasted and double-breasted versions. The double-breasted overcoat, being warmer, is suggested for winterwear. Save the single-breasted for spring and fall.

The conventional "box coat," single-breasted or double-breasted, is your best bet. Camel's hair soils too quickly for regular wear. Shown here with traditional silk scarf.
Barney's New York

In September 1980 an acceptable-quality outercoat cost from $250 to $325.

Fabric

The fabric in a topcoat can weigh as little as 13 ounces, but is usually 15–18 ounces. The fabric in an overcoat is 20–24 ounces.

I would not recommend tweed unless you have an assortment of outercoats. Tweed is associated with the country. For business you are better off with a fabric more suited to business occasions. Tweed topcoats are frequently woven with a bold pattern, but I suggest you avoid any pattern.

Nor do I recommend camel hair, unless you have a collection of coats. A double-breasted camel-hair looks dashing on the shoul-

Sir John Gielgud wearing velvet-collar overcoat—not recommended for business. L. Arnold Weissberger's *Famous Faces*

ders of polo players before and after riding; otherwise, it is not really practical. Since the color is light tan, urban soot will quickly take its toll.

Cashmere is popular with upper-income men, who buy it because it's expensive and feels luxurious. Unfortunately, it wears badly, wrinkles badly, tailors badly, and quickly loses its shape.

Many upper-income executives like fur coats: beaver, mink, raccoon, nutria. This is a no-no in my book, for several reasons:

1. Fur coats are bulky and make a man look fatter than he is.
2. They are heavy and uncomfortable.
3. They are too warm, except in the extremely cold weather found, for example, in Minneapolis or Chicago.

However, cloth coats with fur collars are both attractive and warm. They are flattering and highly recommended. Prices range from $500 to $950.

A minimum inventory would include two overcoats and two topcoats. Your first coat should be an oxford gray overcoat; the second coat, a taupe overcoat (a color similar to a British officer's greatcoat). The two topcoats should follow the same colorations as the overcoats. In addition, you should have one raincoat, perhaps with a zip-out lining.

Hats

At one time in the not-too-distant past, a hat was considered a necessary and desirable accessory. It certainly adds a finishing touch to the military uniform, and in business it sometimes separates "the men from the boys." In recent years, however, the decision to wear a hat has become a matter of choice. Today every other man appears hatless. Yet a hat does help to complete the picture, so if you are considering wearing a hat (I'm never without one, summer, winter, spring, or fall), read on.

You will be well-advised to choose only gray or brown hats, matching the hat to the color of your outercoat or suit. Your hat size is determined by the salesman, and I recommend that you buy your hats in a hat store rather than a department store. Not only

Hats look best worn military style—parallel to ground and no side angle.
L. Arnold Weissberger's *Famous Faces*

will a hat store have a much larger selection of styles, fabrics, and colors, but its salespeople are specialists—they sell only hats. Department-store salespeople frequently move from department to department, and the ability to write up a sales slip is all too often their main area of expertise.

The hat style is determined only by the size and shape of your head and face: the smaller your face, the narrower the brim. The style of the overcoat, width of suit lapel, etc., should not be determining factors. The only criterion should be, "How do I look?"

The traditional business hat is a snap-brim style, made of felt. A ribbon band usually trims the hat. A feather adds a spritely touch. All hats should be worn military-style: straight (no side tilt) and parallel to the ground.

If taken care of properly, hats last a long time. That means

Hats look best worn "straight" and parallel to the ground.
Noel Coward wore hats at a rakish angle—not recommended.
L. Arnold Weissberger's *Famous Faces*

storing them during summer. Do not stack them one on top of another. You can have your hats dry-cleaned if needed, but brush them between wearings.

Despite their current popularity, sportier hats are not appropriate for business wear. They call attention to your clothes—not really the best way to project a serious image. Daniel "Pat" Moynihan, professor, author, and senator, has a double "logo." He not only wears bow ties (tiny bow ties, much too small for his large neck, large face, and tall figure), he also wears handwoven Irish tweed hats—becoming to him, but better suited to the country.

Fur hats—Persian lamb, rabbit, and even mink—are generally becoming to most men and are very practical in colder climates. I like fur hats.

In the summer you might wear a regular Panama in the city,

and in the country a planter's-style Panama (a much larger brim). Planters Panamas originated in the South, because they shade the face from the damaging rays of the sun.

Scarves and Mufflers

A recent fashion look that I particularly take exception to is the long scarf worn over a regular suit jacket with the collar turned up. It serves no function other than a decorative one, and the look is shamefully artificial. It's a fashion that, like the Mao jacket and the leisure suit, will disappear as quickly as it appeared. I recommend that you avoid it just as you would avoid wearing earrings.

Nevertheless, scarves with an outercoat are practical for cold weather. They are made of wool, cashmere, silk, or polyester

Jedd Harris, theatrical producer, squashing his left ear with a derby, and squashing his neck with a tight collar.
L. Arnold Weissberger's *Famous Faces*

Emlyn Williams, famous English actor and author,
wearing a woolen muffler to keep out the chill of a
London winter. Traditional Balmacaan coat with
comfortable raglan shoulders.
L. Arnold Weissberger's *Famous Faces*

blends. Wrapped once or twice around the neck, they add considerable warmth. Stay away from patterns. You may want two solid-
colored scarves, one in the gray family and one in the brown
family.

Boots

Ankle-high boots are another fashion item that seems to have
caught on. These boots are expensive and unfortunately serve no
function whatsoever—and in warm weather, they are downright
uncomfortable.

Western boots also are enjoying a mild popularity. If you're riding the range, wear them; but they're hardly appropriate for city dwellers. Identifying yourself with the newest trend—Western wear, aviator scarves, rumpled "unstructured" sports jackets, etc.—might give the impression that you have a certain insecurity about your own role in life and are still trying to find an identity.

To protect shoes from heavy rain, try a pair of one-size-fits-all rubbers. They are light enough in weight and flexible enough to fit into your attaché case. From time to time you will be faced with a heavy snowfall, in which case you will find rubber galoshes helpful. Although 14 inches high, they are lightweight and easy to snap on. If you find yourself at the office with neither rubbers nor galoshes, phone for a taxi. Rubbers are so inexpensive that it is desirable to have two pairs, one for home and one for the office.

Umbrellas

The important thing about umbrellas is to have one available when you need it. It's easy to carry a furled umbrella when rain is forecast. A furled umbrella, like a cane, adds to the complete look. To be sure you have an umbrella available, keep one in the office and another at home. Even though they are inexpensive, put your name tag on the handle to avoid losing one at the office or at a restaurant.

Gloves

Gloves add a finishing touch, and an executive should have at least two pairs of gloves—one pair in brown, one in gray—for everyday wear. In addition, you may want two pairs of lined leather gloves for very cold weather.

Shoes

Wear brown shoes with brown suits, and black shoes with everything else. Wear only leather, because it is better to invest in quality shoes, both from a functional and from an aesthetic point of view. Synthetic leather creates excessive perspiration—because it does not breathe—and encourages athlete's foot. Patent leather is worn for formal occasions only, not for business.

Loafers, originally designed for weekend loafing, have become an accepted part of the Ivy League business uniform. You may want to keep in mind, however, that laced shoes give more support, are better for walking, and are really more appropriate for business.

I am sometimes asked about cordovan shoes. They really are attractive, but they do complicate color-coordination, being neither black nor brown. They are best worn in place of brown shoes—with a brown suit or beige gabardine slacks. I am also asked about suede shoes. Suede shoes are meant to be worn in the country, as are thicker-soled walking shoes and crepe-soled shoes.

Shoe Maintenance

To prevent leather shoes from cracking, use a little preventive medicine. Before you even wear your new shoes, waterproof them with any one of the silicone water-repellents on the market. Follow instructions carefully; generally, two or three coats are needed to make the shoes totally waterproof. Afterward, apply a coat of saddle soap and buff the shoes thoroughly. Apply a shoe polish after every other wearing. Buff the shoes with a soft cloth if you don't polish them.

Avoid self-cleaning shoe polish, since prolonged use may cause the leather to crack—at least that has been my experience.

Use wooden shoe trees, which let your shoes breathe. Avoid plastic shoe trees.

16

Weekends Are Important Too

ONE Saturday, Anthony Bergamo, The Custom Shop's executive vice-president, along with Mrs. Bergamo, treated me and Mrs. Levitt to lunch at the Plaza Hotel. He had reserved a table for four at the Edwardian Room, whose handsome, old-world decor and oversized windows overlooking Central Park and Fifth Avenue's Fountain Plaza make it one of the world's finest restaurant settings. The maitre d' took our lunch order and while we were waiting for the first course, I glanced idly around the room. It was late May and I was surprised to see how many of the luncheon guests looked like "blue collar" workers on a lunch break. Properly selected casual attire is very flattering. Yet most of the men (and some of the women) had obviously given no thought to dressing for the weekend.

If you look like an executive during the week, you should look like an executive on weekends. Some men—too many really—give so little attention to their weekend wardrobe that they actually wind up by presenting a "blue collar" image.

Before getting down to specifics, let's start with the most important general area—*color!* And let's make it easy by starting with *monochromatic* color schemes, or ensembles consisting of only one color, be it different shades of browns and tans, or navy and blues, or black, grays, and white. Everything must be included in the monochrome scheme. Shoes, slacks, shirts, blazers, sport jackets, sweaters, jackets, hats, gloves, topcoats, car coats, windbreakers, raincoats—everything and anything you buy should be colored to go with a monochromatic ensemble.

After your monochromatic ensembles have been *completed*, it is relatively easy to introduce a single accent color. If clothes are a nuisance, forget the accent color. I know one thing for sure: You will be surprised at how much better the clothes you now own look once you have grouped and worn them *strictly* by color.

There are weekends and then there are weekends. In the main, your outfits should consist of the items listed above, plus the clothes you need for active sports—sailing, riding, tennis, beaching, skiing, golf, gardening, etc. And you should have clothes for cocktail parties, lunch parties, dinner parties, clambakes, etc. Happily you will be able to wear most of your clothes year-round. A few items obviously will be reserved for the appropriate season.

Sport Jackets and Blazers

You need a minimum of one navy blazer and one strongly patterned tweed jacket. There is a difference between a blazer and a sport jacket. The blazer, like the full-dress uniform of a naval officer, has gold buttons. The sport jacket, in contrast, has bone buttons—the same buttons used on a regular suit. Extra-sporty jackets have leather buttons. Some tweeds are very loosely woven and as a result wear out at the elbow. Because one English country gentleman, a member of the nobility, hated to part with an old sport jacket and so elected to preserve the jacket by placing suede patches on the elbows, a new fashion was born—a fashion that by now has worked its way through the classes to the masses.

At cocktail parties or dinner parties you'll be expected to wear a blazer, shirt, and tie. If it is less formal omit the tie. But do not spread the shirt collar outside the collar or lapels of your blazer: that's considered high fashion only in Moscow. If you want to be daring, open up the collar and three buttons of your shirt, but keep the collar points inside the blazer.

Most summer evenings are cool enough so that one can be comfortable in a flannel blazer. But for daytime a tropical-weight blazer is desirable. White, pink, yellow, or tan linen blazers can

The traditional navy blazer, this time with white pearl buttons instead of gold, and white flannels instead of gray flannels.
Barney's New York

be worn during the day and/or for any evening occasion. Single-breasted lightweights may be preferable to double-breasted for daytime wear, because they are cooler.

Slacks

For starters, forget jeans. They have become a cliché and are better suited to cowboys, plumbers, and ex–flower children. If you are reading this book, you may already have outgrown jeans. They wrinkle badly, have no finish at the bottom, hang without grace, and are unflattering to any man with a waist measurement over 30. The myth that they are comfortable to wear is just that— a myth. Fashionably cut jeans are binding in all the wrong places. Standing may be okay, but when one sits down—well, who needs it?

A classic wardrobe has slacks in gray flannel and tan gabardine, both of which can be worn year-round. If you spend much

139

Wear the yellow linen blazer as a change from navy blue.

time in the country, you may also need solid-color slacks to coordinate with an existing tweed jacket: for example, navy slacks for a predominantly blue plaid or tweed. If you spend entire summers in the country, you should have slacks in white, red, yellow, and sail blue. For working around the house, try tan chinos instead of jeans.

If you are a swinging single or even part of a swinging couple, you could dazzle friends with black or purple velveteen slacks. Forget corduroy. Corduroy is too stiff and drapes badly. Velveteen drapes well and is soft to the touch.

Shirts

Oxford cloth is the basic for country shirts, in shades of blue, tan, pink, and white. End-on-end broadcloth, a stand-in for oxford, is priced about 20 percent higher. Tattersall checks and ginghams are also popular in all colors. Solid-color country shirts are frequently made with epaulettes.

Some men wear flannel shirts in the fall and winter, but I find them most uncomfortable, both because they itch and because they

The Oxford shirt worn under a crew-neck sweater, the classic look on campus and off. Bold pattern tweed jacket Barney's New York

are bulky. Equally bad, they are unbecoming because they are usually made in strong, dark colors that drain the color from a face that is already drained of the color acquired by summer sun. Oxford cotton shirts are more comfortable next to the body and more flattering to the complexion. Therefore, instead of expensive flannel shirts, I recommend oxford shirts worn under crew-neck sweaters. Remember: "Pale shades add color to the face; dark shades drain the color."

Knitwear

The turtleneck is popular and is becoming to most men. Pale shades (beige, gray, white, light blue) are more becoming than dark shades. Even if you have no belly, the turtleneck looks better

The turtleneck looks better under a car coat than a jacket.
Barney's New York

worn outside your slacks. It is *not* flattering when worn with a blazer or sport jacket, although it looks fine with a car coat or poplin windbreaker.

The pullover Lacoste shirt—the half-sleeve shirt with the alligator on the chest—has become almost a uniform. It comes in twenty different shades, requires little or no ironing, and because it is knitted, resists wrinkling.

Sweaters

The crew-neck sweater, like the Lacoste knit shirt, has become a uniform. A good store will have them in lamb's wool in fifteen or twenty different colors.

If you are *really* slender, you may want to include in your country wardrobe a bulky, hand-knitted sweater—most of them are done abroad, many in Ireland.

142

As I said before, summer nights are frequently cool and a lamb's wool or shetland crewneck sweater is comfortable to wear over an oxford shirt for the movies, an evening walk, or informal get-togethers.

Shoes

In warm weather, many men wear tennis sneakers as a catch-all, even though there are good-looking casual shoes that are more fun to wear. Get yourself a pair of white shoes, and a pair in tan. There are also sandals, as well as espadrilles from Spain. Each year produces a new series of inexpensive and attractive sport shoes.

For social occasions, you may want loafers, one pair in black and one pair in tan, with leather soles. Also get leather shoes with thick rubber soles, for walking and rainy weather.

Laced-up hiking shoes (if you've been in the army, you know what I mean) are practical and much-needed shoes for a man who likes to walk in the country. They give necessary support for long walks and help to avoid sprained ankles when walking on rough terrain. They are frequently made of unfinished cowhide to better camouflage dust from the road.

Outerjackets

You will also want a poplin zippered jacket with a stand-up mandarin-type collar (almost has the effect of the white collar worn by the clergy). The poplin jacket has roomy pockets and is usually worn with slacks and turtleneck—or, better yet, a regular shirt with the collar points showing over a lamb's wool crewneck sweater.

The sheepskin coat is very popular, but I give it four demerits:

1. Having no silk-lined sleeves, it is uncomfortable to put on and uncomfortable to take off.
2. It adds an extra fifteen or twenty pounds to a man's appearance because it looks so bulky.

The traditional poplin jacket, a handy garment usable summer, winter, spring, and fall.
New Process Company

3. Like all leather garments, it is uncomfortable to wear, because unlike cloth, it has no give. More, it's impractical because it weathers badly when caught in the rain.
4. It costs more than it is worth—it is expensive but looks inexpensive.

A better bet, in my opinion, is a full-length or knee-length raglan-sleeve tweed overcoat—with a fur collar if you can afford it, a pile collar if you can't. Brooks Brothers has been selling a pile-collar tweed coat since forever. The raglan sleeve is more comfortable and a pile lining gives you warmth without weight.

Add a knee-length car coat. Car coats come in corduroy and poplin, sometimes with a detachable pile lining. They come with or without hoods and with or without fur collars.

*The sheep-lined jacket—bulky, expensive, uncomfortable,
very popular—not recommended.*
Barney's New York

Since brown is a popular color for countrywear, you may
want to consider beige as the most practical color. You might also
want a hip-length jacket. If your car coat is corduroy, your hip-
length jacket could be poplin, and vice versa.

Wear the car coat in the spring and fall, the tweed raglan-
sleeve overcoat in the winter.

Weekend Social

Listed below are several suggestions for those social occasions
that are a regular part of married life. Social occasions in the country call for clothes less formal than those worn in the city, the

major difference being blazers, sport jackets, and loafers instead of suits and laced shoes.

Summer Lunch

White slacks with a white or yellow knitted pullover, worn outside. Try a yellow belt, yellow espadrilles, no socks. You might carry a yellow dacron/linen blazer with white buttons. Traditional sunglasses.

Early Evening Cookout

Depending on the temperature and the location, wear slacks —gray flannel, beige gabardine, or beige tropical (at the beach, chinos). A pullover knit shirt in the same color (beige with beige, or gray with gray). Or try gray flannel slacks and, if you have a fresh sunburn, a navy pullover. Stay away from red, rust, orange, dark green, or purple shirts, because they all drain color from your face. Wear suede or leather loafers; at the beach, wear rubber-soled sport shoes.

For cooler weather, wear gray flannel slacks, a blue oxford shirt, and a gray lamb's-wool crew-neck sweater with the shirt collar outside the sweater. If the weather is cooler still, add a navy blazer or a beige poplin windbreaker.

Dinner Party

Your hostess will be pleased if you appear in traditional slacks, loafers, an oxford shirt, a bow tie, and a blazer. If you can't tie a bow tie, our illustration makes it easy. An alternate costume could be a tweed sport jacket. As a rule, sport jackets tend to be less flattering than the blazer, because they are more bulky. Color-coordination is also more difficult, because the jackets are apt to be colorful.

Bow ties are attractive for country weekends. If your tweed jacket has a definite pattern, wear a solid-color shantung bow tie and a solid-color shirt that picks up the colors in the jacket.

I hope you don't get the impression from the foregoing that a large investment is necessary. Compared with what you are spending right now on automobiles, liquor, vacations, etc., we are talking about very little. As these clothes are all classics, you will have them for years.

Sporting Clothes

If you enjoy sports, why not have the fun of looking the part? In one hour you can write up your inventory and make an "open to buy" list for shopping.

TENNIS: I play tennis six mornings a week every summer and two mornings a week every winter (on an indoor court). One morning this past winter, I arrived twenty minutes early and had occasion to watch the other players as they trickled in for their 9:00 A.M. games. They were paying $18 an hour for the court, most of them playing two and three times a week; obviously, they were pretty secure in their jobs or pretty well fixed.

The lineup of tattletale gray, wrinkled, ill-assorted, ill-fitting tennis clothes, finished off with seemingly unwashed faces and uncombed hair, was surprising. I was reminded of our own children (they grew up in the 1960s), who prepared themselves for bed by dropping their clothes on the bedroom floor. The next morning

Alan King wearing his "Planter's Panama"—a flattering summer look.
L. Arnold Weissberger's *Famous Faces*

147

they picked them off the floor and put them back on. Regardless of their ability to play or pay, the image projected by these avid tennis players was one of poverty and incompetence.

When tennis first became popular as a television attraction, designers and manufacturers sought to increase sales by adding color. They totally overlooked the fact that tennis is a summer sport played frequently under a blazing sun, and traditionally in white clothes. White has two functions: First of all, white reflects the rays of the sun, whereas colored shirts absorb the rays; white is cool, colors are hot. Secondly, white is more flattering, because it complements a suntan. If you have any doubts about the validity of these observations, just observe how dirty most of our male tennis champions look the next time you see them on television.

I recommend a white knitted pullover, a good-quality lisle T-shirt with a boatneck—preferably with no collar, because the collar wilts so quickly. Pull the shirt down tautly inside snug-fitting bikini underwear. A bikini holds the genitals more comfortably than the conventional jockstrap and will also hold down the tennis shirt. Tennis shirts look better worn inside tennis shorts.

White socks, a white headband or a white peak to keep the sun out of the eyes, white shoes, and white sweatbands on the wrists complete the outfit. To warm up before play begins and to avoid a charley horse after play ends, the traditional white cable-stitch V-neck pullover with the traditional navy-and-red contrasting stripes makes even a hacker look like a tennis player.

Tennis whites should look white. They are now being made in polyester. See Chapter 19 on laundry care for washing of tennis whites.

GOLF: A golfing outfit is really easy to assemble, the key being color-coordination. If your shoes are brown, wear chino slacks (tan color) made of dacron and cotton. They are washable and require little or no pressing. Wear a tan half-sleeve, Lacoste-type knit shirt made of cotton, or dacron and cotton. If you want a dash of color, try a bright red belt. In cooler weather, add a tan poplin hip-length, zippered jacket. If you want to keep the sun out of your eyes, wear a tan poplin, snap-brim hat; or if you are especially sensitive to sun, wear a tan poplin "baseball" hat with a large peak.

If your shoes are black, wear the same outfit as above, except in gray. Generally speaking, however, a beige color is more flattering to the complexion.

In cool weather, switch to gray flannel slacks and wear a long-sleeve shetland pullover over a half-sleeve cotton knit.

Most important, make sure your knit shirt fits on the easy side. Unless you have the build of an Adonis, a tight-fitting shirt is sure to make you look fatter than you are. And don't overlook the fact that *all* shirts will shrink.

SUIT SIZE	KNIT SHIRT SIZE
34–36	S
38–40	M
42–44	L
46–48	XL

BOATING: Because boating is generally a midsummer sport, white is again the best color. White ducks, white sailor pants, or white shorts with a white knit shirt are all suitable for fair weather. For bad weather, wear the traditional "foul weather" gear, usually in bright yellow. The trousers are generally fastened like pajamas, with their own cord. The top of foul-weather gear has its own hood, and when it is properly fastened, you are completely covered in a relatively light, bright, attractive outfit.

GARDENING: I have never understood the fascination for this back-breaking activity, so I have only one recommendation for gardeners: wear a large white hat to deflect the sun's rays from the *back* of the head and *back* of the neck.

A Typical Day

Perhaps you might find this discussion more interesting if I were to tell you how I dress for my own weekend activities. I will recount a typical Friday night and Saturday during the summer.

On Friday nights, we frequently go to a film. Because movie

houses are air conditioned and usually quite cool, I wear slacks and a pullover lisle shirt. I always take along a wool sweater or jacket and usually wear solid-color sport socks with rubber-soled sports shoes.

Saturday morning I am on my tennis court from 9:00 to 11:00. You already know what my tennis outfit looks like—white shorts, white lisle pullover, white socks, white tennis sneakers, and wristband. I then take a shower, swim in the pool, and have lunch in a Japanese-style kimono.

I leave home at 2:00 to go sailing, dressing in shorts or white sailor pants with either nothing on top or, sometimes, a half-sleeved pullover (in colder weather, a long-sleeved pullover). After returning from sailing, I take a nap before dressing for a dinner party. If I am the host, I am apt to be less formal than if I am a guest.

A Final Word

If I were to give one last word of advice, it would be to keep country clothes simple, and your color-coordination simple as possible. Stay with one base color as much as is practicable. If you are wearing brown shoes, let everything be in the brown family. If you are wearing white shoes, let everything be white with the possible exception of one bright accent color.

17

"Le Smoking"—Les Big Nights

IN Brooklyn it's called a tuxedo; in Paris, *le smoking;* in London, a dinner jacket; and on Park Avenue, black tie. Given this wide range of labels, it is not surprising that I am asked so many questions regarding appropriate attire for formal wear.

There is really not much to say, except to underline a principle, "Simplicity is elegance, and the soul of elegance is simplicity." Stay away from velvet collars, velvet dinner jackets, lacy evening shirts, brocaded evening shirts, evening shirts with ruffles down the front, evening shirts with ruffled sleeves, evening shirts with fly fronts, and evening shirts with button-down collars (still being worn by a few hard-line Ivy Leaguers). Avoid blue evening shirts; they are essential for television appearances, but otherwise you'll look better in white.

Barring a *drastic* weight change, you will have your evening clothes forever. It's the one time you want to leave your home feeling right, and it pays to invest in a complete ensemble, an ensemble that does you justice.

A dinner jacket is black with satin or grosgrain lapels and a matching stripe on the outside of each trouser leg. The traditional evening shirt has a pleated bosom of white broadcloth with a voile or batiste body cloth for cooler comfort. Pleats vary from a quarter-inch to three-quarters of an inch. There is a 1½-inch top center with double buttonholes to allow for studs, and French cuffs to allow for matching cuff links.

Leonard Bernstein, brilliant composer, conductor, and concert pianist loves clothes and wears them well. On formal occasions he frequently sports an opera cape. In this picture he is wearing the typical Austrian vest under his dinner jacket.
L. Arnold Weissberger's *Famous Faces*

The butterfly bow tie is popular and becoming. If the lapels are satin, look for a satin bow; if the lapels are grosgrain, try to find a grosgrain bow. Avoid velvet bow ties. Your bow tie will look better if you tie it yourself, because ready-made clip-ons look artificial and tend to distort the shirt collar. If you don't know how to tie a bow, I suggest that you do your practicing before the important evening.

By all means wear studs. Tiffany has them in gold for $1,000, but Swank has them in comparable goldplate sets that cost only $10 to $20. Simple gold or black onyx studs are best.

Formal clothes are usually worn with lightweight over-the-calf socks, patent leather pumps, black vest, or cummerbund.

I am sometimes asked if it is permissible to wear a white turtleneck with formal clothes. The answer to that one is *no*—that's yet another example of the fashion world's influence.

Anthony Armstrong-Jones, an English photographer, achieved worldwide notoriety when he took unto himself a wife, Princess Margaret of England. Thus endowed, he became Lord Snowdon. He was a photographer who believed himself to be an artist. Like

See how much better Mr. Shapiro looks. His collar fits, he is showing cuff at the wrist, he is wearing three plains, and looks the way the chairman of the board of Du Pont should look.

many artists, he called attention to himself not only through his work but also through an idiosyncratic flouting of convention. Snowdon appeared at a dinner party wearing a white silk turtleneck with his dinner jacket. He was widely photographed and for one season only, dinner jackets and white turtlenecks were seen at some of our best dinner parties. If a man were to appear at a formal affair today wearing a white silk turtleneck with formal clothes, he would be marked "hicktown." There is really nothing "squarer" than a high-fashion style whose time has come and gone.

I have also been questioned about white tie and tails and cutaways (morning coats). White tie is often referred to as "full dress." The shirt has a stiff bosom with heavily starched link cuffs. You cannot wear the same shirt for black tie and white tie: White tie calls for a separate wing collar that is then attached to a neckband shirt. You will not receive many invitations calling for white tie, unless you are in the State Department. And if you do, you will always find a sprinkling of men wearing black tie. White tie is essential only for diplomats, concert artists, symphony conductors, and professional dancers—and perhaps for chairmen of conglomerates.

If you are going to wear white tie, do it correctly, because you will be in prestigious company. A separate stiff-wing collar is a must, and there is a loop on the back of the neckband that prevents the bow tie from sliding too far up on the shirt collar in back. You should also wear a silk top hat, and obviously a white vest.

Like white tie and tails, cutaway coats, worn for afternoon weddings, are usually rented, both for the groom and for the ushers, and paid for by the bride's mother. The less said about this custom the better—the whole business is barbaric. That is, except for the divorce, which, in today's society, is a fairly civilized ceremony.

In winter you will need an outercoat. Avoid tweed! Try a white scarf, black hat, black gloves, and furled umbrella. If you are obliged to wear a tan raincoat, try a lame excuse such as "a late newsflash predicted rain for tonight."

The cutaway, usually rented
for formal afternoon weddings.
If your lovely daughter insists,
how can you say no?
After Six

An appropriate overcoat for formal occasions.
Barney's New York

18

New Concepts about Accessories

CHAIRMAN Mao never claimed credit for saying, "A chain is as strong as its weakest link." Nevertheless, that principle applies to your complete wardrobe, and as long as we have gone this far, let's finish the picture with a few pointers you may want to consider in the matter of accessories.

Socks

You will need solid-color socks in black, oxford gray, and brown. In summer, wear tan, blue, and white. And even if your wife knits them specially for you, avoid patterned socks.

Socks should fit over the calf. It's a real turn-off to see a patch of hairy skin visible between the tops of anklets and the bottoms of trousers. Over-the-calf socks are self-supporting.

I had never really understood why certain men don't wear over-the-calf hose until one night, at a small dinner party, I learned the reason. One of my guests wore expensive clothes but ankle-length socks. When I asked him why, he said, "Because over-the-calf socks keep falling down." That may have been true years ago, when socks were made with a two-inch elasticized top, but today, Burlington Mills, among others, makes over-the-calf socks that are elasticized all the way. You have a choice of cotton or wool, both of which are blended with Spandex for elasticity. This new breed of sock stays up for the life of the hose.

Burlington Mills also has come up with another innovation: socks that are guaranteed to eliminate foot odor. These socks are easily identified by a green stripe knitted across the toes. They are available in all-cotton, all-polyester, all-wool, or any of the three blended with polyester. One size fits all, and they are advantageously priced. They are available in regular-length and over-the-calf length. Having tried the rest, I find these to be best.

Belts

I recommend wearing slacks with belt loops, because belts add still another finishing touch. Here again, you need a minimum of two belts, black and brown. The width you select will depend upon the width of your belt loops. Avoid using a thin belt with wide belt loops.

A six-pound fluctuation in weight will change your waistline by one inch. One advantage of a belt over beltless trousers is the possibility of adjusting the belt to accommodate a change in the waistline.

There is another advantage to wearing belts. Like many men, I have a tendency to overeat, and when I get up from a table, or sometimes while I am still at the table, I can discreetly let out one notch on the belt—after which I breathe a gentle sigh of relief.

Attaché Cases

For business, you should use an attaché case rather than a briefcase. Placed on your lap, the attaché case can be used as a portable desk when you are traveling. Invest in a good-quality attaché case: It's the one accessory that will be spotted immediately.

Wallets

I don't carry a wallet, because wallets are too bulky; they stretch my suit out of shape and therefore put me out of shape.

Anything that needs to be carried in a wallet can just as easily be carried in my attaché case or the glove compartment of my car. I carry bills in my right-hand trouser pocket, folded over my American Express card. Keys are in my left-hand pocket on a key chain. All other credit cards, my driver's license, and pictures of my wife and children are in my attaché case, as are my reserve eyeglasses. In other words, there is no visible bulk anywhere in my clothing.

I strongly urge that you go without a wallet or an address book in a pocket (my address book is also kept in my attaché case).

Handkerchiefs

I recommend using pure linen handkerchiefs. Linen is more absorbent, and the quality is immediately apparent. Have your handkerchiefs monogrammed. Why not? You will only wear out about five handkerchiefs a year, and a monogrammed linen handkerchief can be bought for about $4. Once again—a finishing touch that projects the right image.

Do *not* use yesterday's messed-up handkerchief.

Pocket Squares

Silk foulard squares add a dressy touch for the man who really wears his clothes well. Such a man is generally good-looking, casual, and carries his clothes with a certain air. Cary Grant and former New York City mayor John Lindsay are two good examples. I have tried pocket squares, but even though I carry clothes well, I have never been comfortable with a handkerchief in my breast pocket, so I don't wear one. If you like the look, however, I have three suggestions you may want to consider:

1. Don't use white linen.
2. If you are wearing three plains, wear a silk pattern that contains the base color and the accent color of your ensemble.
3. If you are wearing two plains and a pattern, use a solid-silk pocket square that matches the accent color of your ensemble.

Jewelry

There is not much that can be said about men's jewelry, except:

1. A wedding band on the left hand adds substance and keeps a married man free of undesirable entanglements.
2. A ring on the little finger—for example, a gold ring with black onyx—is decorative. However, a gold ring with a diamond looks better on a woman's hand. If you own one, this is the perfect time to sell it.
3. Cuff links and collar pins add a nice finishing touch, as do identification bracelets. All should be gold if you can afford it, gold-filled if you cannot.
4. In the 1960s, flower children and hippies went to great pains to adorn themselves. Having little real cash to spend on clothes, they took their cues from the American Indian and turned to paint and beads. In the 1970s the beads turned to necklaces for men, with various symbols proclaiming their faith: the cross, the Star of David, the fertility symbol, the Hebrew letter meaning "life," etc. Body jewelry was displayed in Harry Belafonte fashion: a sport shirt worn open to the navel. It's a nice look for hippies but a fashion that is frowned upon at the better country clubs.

Ascots

The ascot is a classic weekend look that originated in England and it has survived all the fads. An ascot or a silk square folded like an ascot is used to "dress up" an open-necked sport shirt. Unfortunately the ascot, being made of silk, keeps moving. You may leave your home with it perfectly arranged and by the time you have arrived, its look may have changed completely. There are two ways that problem can be handled:

1. Before you put on your shirt, use a small safety pin to attach the ascot to the back of the neckband of your shirt collar. This anchors it.

2. After you have the shirt on and the ascot tied, use a second safety pin on the ascot only, to prevent it from becoming untied.

This brings us to the end of discussion about the money you'll be spending to buy things. So now let's look at the money you'll be spending to maintain the things you have bought.

Cris Alexander, actor and photographer. In Europe, sport shirts usually sport an ascot.
L. Arnold Weissberger's *Famous Faces*

19

As with Your Cars—Maintenance Is Essential

Suits, Blazers, and Slacks

Suits should be professionally cleaned, but usually not more than twice a year. Actually, if you rotate your suits and brush them before each wearing, once a year may be sufficient. Better suits are hand-pressed (also called underpressing) many, many times in the process of being manufactured. Machine pressing, which most cleaners offer, is apt to put a *jacket* out of shape. Therefore, too-frequent cleaning or pressing of your jackets is neither necessary nor desirable.

Certain precautionary measures will eliminate the need for frequent dry cleaning. After wearing a suit, hang it on a "valet" to air overnight. The next morning, before putting it in the closet, hang the suit on a wishbone-type wooden suit-hanger to help it retain its shape. Trousers should hang on special trouser hangers, to give the wrinkles a chance to "unwrinkle." Wear your suits in an actual sequence by rotating them regularly.

If your suit has an odor after being dry-cleaned, switch to another cleaner. It means that the cleaner uses *old* solvent.

Take suits for cleaning in April/May or September/October. That's when summer clothes are brought out or put away.

The Greatest Sin of All

It is extraordinary how many executives save pennies by having their wives do their shirts. This places a needless burden on the wife, but even worse, it's a personal put-down. Puckering on the collar, cuffs, and shirt front project an image of a clerk, surely not an executive. If you feel it's important to save $3 a week on laundry, cut down elsewhere because your business uniform is important, almost as important as your degree. If you don't project the image of an executive it may never occur to the CEO that you really are one.

People are so foolish about money! Here is an example, taken from Scott Spencer's novel *Endless Love*. You just know this woman is for real:

> I learned to walk away from many luxuries—and each child caused me to evacuate another set of expensive yearnings. Yet the one that would never die (I protected it like an endangered species) was my love for expensive chocolate. It survived my love for well-made books, magazine subscriptions, alligator purses, and English cigarettes; the chocolate survived turquoise and gold, as well as the simpler pleasures of a first-run movie or sending the shirts out to the Chinese laundry. . . .

The character in this novel speaks for millions and millions of upper- and middle-class Americans who think sending shirts to the laundry is a luxury. How extraordinary to find a $3-per-week laundry charge (five shirts at 60¢ each) listed as a luxury along with alligator purses ($500–$1,000 each), English cigarettes ($2.50 a pack), Godiva chocolates ($14.00 a pound), etc.

I strongly recommend that you send your shirts to a laundry. For $150 a year, you can send all your shirts out, and it's well worth it, because a shirt laundered at home never has the crisp look of a professionally laundered shirt. An unpressed shirt is a personal put-down, more suited to a clerk than an executive. No one will say your shirt has not been pressed, but a colleague will sense, without realizing why, that your image is decidedly not first class.

Some men use an "excuse" for saving that weekly $3: "The laundry ruins my shirts." So, let's examine the actual cost. Our customers wear out only four shirts a year because custom-made shirts do wear longer. Now, assuming that you order four shirts a year at $25, for a total of $100, and assuming that the laundering *is* tough on shirts—that a poor laundry cuts the wear by 10%—that would cost you $10 a year or, at 20%, $20. Ten or twenty dollars a year is negligible for a man in your position (and I do have some small idea of your status because you are reading these pages). I suggest that you forget about wear and maintenance because that is the wrong place for a man in your position to economize. Your image is important and consequential; don't put it down.

To find the best laundry, use the trial-and-error method. Try four or five laundries listed in the Yellow Pages and select the one that gives you the best value—value being composed of quality, service and price. If you are fortunate enough to have a Chinese laundry in your neighborhood, you will find that it is apt to be your best bet.

Although most laundries know better, and although the label attached to the shirt will be marked "Do not bleach," it is your responsibility to call the laundry's attention to the fact that cream-colored shirts ("color of silk") or light blue shirts must *never* be washed with white shirts. Bleach is used to make white shirts look whiter than white. But bleach acts as a dye on colored shirts—it changes the color, and always for the worse. Tattletale gray, usually seen with polyester or 65/35 blends, is a sure sign that an improper detergent was used.

Starch or No Starch

As a general rule, thin men look better with the lightest possible starch in their collars (collars always require some starch). A light starch doesn't really feel like starch; it adds a firm finish to the collar and prevents unnecessary wrinkling. Fat men, on the other hand, look better in collars that are starched medium to heavy.

Home Laundering of Shirts

Shirts laundered at home generally look pretty bad—awful, actually. However, if you insist on doing shirts at home, the following information will help. A well-pressed cotton shirt collar makes all the difference between the way you should look and the way too many men do look.

White Shirts and Cream Shirts

1. There are two kinds of bleach: chlorine and nonchlorine. If you use a chlorine bleach on a white polyester shirt, the white will discolor—that is, it will become tattletale gray. If your white shirt became tattletale gray because an improper bleach was used, this can be corrected by soaking overnight in a solution of one cup of a dishwashing-machine compound (Calgonite) per gallon of warm water. Then, without drying, wash the shirt in a regular automatic wash cycle.
2. White shirts must never be washed with cream-colored shirts.
3. Cream-colored shirts must be washed with colored shirts.

Damaging the Fabric

If a drop of undiluted bleach falls on your shirt, it will cause a "bleach burn." After several washings, there will be small holes in the fabric.

Home Ironing/Pressing

It is not hard to iron a shirt if you know how—in which case, you can pass the information on to your wife, mistress, or housekeeper.

1. Dip the collars and cuffs in Niagara liquid starch solution, or a similar product. Squeeze out excess moisture and allow the shirt to dry. The starch bottle gives the ratio of water to starch for a light, medium, or heavy result. I suggest light starch.
2. Always use a steam iron and/or a "spray mister."
3. Press the *wrong* side of the collar first. When you turn the collar over and press the right side, all puckering will disappear. Start at the collar point and press toward the center. Then start at the other point and press to the center.
4. To get the puckering out of the front and cuffs, press the reverse side first, then press the right side.

164

5. When pressing any part of the shirt, pull the fabric as you iron.
6. As a final step, fold the collar with your hands, then press it only at the center. This will create a graceful "roll." Carefully button the first *two* buttons of the shirt and place on a hanger.

20

Men's Liberation Includes Some "Makeup"

GROOMING may be thought of as a woman's province, but if you consider the time and care that men spend with their blow dryers, it becomes immediately apparent that they also care very much about how they look. It is the pulled-together, well-groomed man, from the top of his cared-for hair to the shine on his always-polished shoes, who projects an image of success and of well-being. So, let's look at men's options.

Skin Care

Do you look better with a suntan? Most men do. Unfortunately, suntan is the most common cause of skin cancer. Suntan also leads to premature aging and wrinkles, and it gives your skin a leathery look.

A fresh suntan is always becoming, but after two weeks, the tan turns a yellowish brown, a color that is not becoming. On the other hand, city pallor, a look familiar to most urban dwellers, is not becoming either. All women know this and use makeup to compensate.

Happily, there is a new product for men that offers the advantage of a fresh suntan with none of the disadvantages: the so-called bronzing gels marketed by Estée Lauder's "Clinique" and by Revlon. Aside from making you look better, they are also skin moisturizers, guaranteed (according to the ads) to retard aging. Properly applied, bronzing gels *never* look artificial, because the "gel" is totally invisible.

My best advice, however, is moderation. Use the bronzer *lightly* and on the forehead, nose, and cheekbones *only*. Don't try for a look that says you've just returned from two weeks in Palm Beach. On the contrary, make it look as though you had taken a one-hour walk on a sunny day in May. The result will be a slight redness on your forehead, nose, and cheekbones.

Finally, take a tip from your barber, who applies talcum with a towel after shaving you. Apply face powder with a powder puff (not too much) and you'll see the difference for yourself. Gel and face powder, properly handled, never look artificial.

Hair Care

Hair has always been a problem—and frequently a problem of too little, too soon. In spite of all the magic potions peddled throughout the ages, there is little that can be done about baldness. But men with unruly hair also have a problem.

Women have used blow dryers for years and now men use them too. Improperly used, however, they create an artificial look: Too many television announcers look as if they are wearing wigs. If possible, avoid using a blow dryer, because excessive use of a blow dryer may be hard on the hair. If your hair is difficult to manage, experiment with several hair stylists until you find a simple hairstyle that is becoming, natural looking, and easy to take care of.

A visit to your barber every three weeks should keep you looking the way you want to look.

Facial Hair

Most men should avoid moustaches, long sideburns, and beards. If a man with a low forehead wears facial hair, he begins to look like an ape man.

Long sideburns are not becoming to men with round faces,

high cheekbones, bald heads, and/or long faces. Long sideburns make a fat face look fatter; they also call attention to baldness *because* of the contrast. Long sideburns smother high cheekbones —an asset that should be highlighted. A man with a long face should avoid long sideburns, because they tend to make the face look even longer. Finally, long sideburns look mildly villainous or shady.

Moustaches look best on men with long faces, but the Oriental moustache should be avoided because it gives the wearer an unhappy, even sinister look. In contrast, the moustache popular with British Army officers gives an upbeat image, because it goes up at the ends instead of down.

Beards are better left to artists, writers, psychiatrists, professors and scientists, advertising and public relations executives. Although a beard may be acceptable to 60 percent of your clients

Louis Calhern, screen star, wearing a traditional "British Colonel" mustache—a big improvement over the Fu Manchu mustaches made popular in the Seventies.
L. Arnold Weissberger's *Famous Faces*

and colleagues, it may possibly cause the other 40 percent a certain uneasiness. Why risk turning off that 40 percent?

Fingernails

Hands are highly visible at any business meeting. There is one way and only one way to maintain clean fingernails: use a nailbrush twice a day. I do not recommend highly polished nails, but if you know nothing about nail care, it might be advisable to have your nails manicured several times, to see how good they can look.

Nails that are prone to splitting, cracking, or breaking off may be a sign of a vitamin deficiency, so you may want to have your diet checked by a doctor. In the meantime, there are several clear "nail-hardening enamels" that will prevent splitting; one such, widely advertised, is Sally Hanson's "Hard as Nails."

Breath

If your business requires face-to-face contact, and it usually does, I suggest that you avoid eating foods that contain garlic—pickles, salamis, garlic in salad dressing, and most delicatessen meats. Avoid eating raw onions. Garlic and onion odors cannot be masked by chewing gum or mouthwash, because the offensive (to me) odor comes from the stomach, not the mouth.

There are two other reasons for bad breath. One is improperly cleaned teeth. An electric toothbrush does a better job than a regular toothbrush. But even an electric toothbrush won't get out the food particles that collect between your teeth. Therefore, my dentist recommends using "stim-u-dents" every night. They work like dental floss but are much, much easier to use.

The second reason for bad breath is indigestion. This can be partially overcome by taking antacid pills and by brushing your *tongue*, but a more intelligent approach would be to avoid eating foods that cause indigestion.

A third reason for bad breath is poor gums. If your gums bleed, see a dentist.

Finally, alcohol on the breath when coming back from lunch may project an "over the hill" image.

Scents

Most men use an underarm deodorant. I don't recommend a spray deodorant, because it tends to have an "afterscent." Use only *unscented* roll-ons. The function of the deodorant is to retard perspiration; if you want a fragrance, buy it separately. The fragrance used in a deodorant is the cheapest quality, not worthy of your eminence.

If you do wear a scent, use it sparingly and change scents frequently—friends and colleagues should not smell you coming. Fragrance must never touch *any* article of clothing—not shirt, not underwear, not suit—because fragrance on fabric quickly goes stale, and stale fragrance is unpleasant. If stale odor gets into your clothes, it is difficult to get it out. So it's best to avoid using a spray. Better to place a single drop of fragrance on your fingertip; touch each ear lobe and the back of the other hand.

Shoe Care

It is obvious that shoes should be polished, but the days of the 10¢ shoeshine are gone and bootblacks are not found on every corner, so most men have their own shoeshine kits.

Color coordination carries through to your shoes. Remember: wear brown shoes with brown suits and black shoes with everything else.

The Seven-Minute Grooming Stretch

The daily attention you give to grooming will make you look your best and make you feel good about yourself. The time required is minimal—an extra minute or two every morning is important if you are career-minded.

Another point: If you are going out at night directly from the office, it's desirable to shave and change to a clean shirt. This gives you an "up" feeling and helps you enjoy yourself that much more. If you are taking a night off to forget taxes, inflation, and the Bomb, go all the way—dress up!

21

Tips, Probably More Productive Than Those Received from Your Broker

APPROPRIATE attire is obviously desirable, but executives are also judged by their "social behavior." So let's look at some of the other things that were left out of the MBA curriculum:

1. If the president or ranking officer of your company doesn't smoke, it would be good manners and good business not to smoke in his presence. The same would be true when spending time with a nonsmoking client.

2. Recent statistics indicate that only one adult out of four smokes cigarettes. Ever since airlines set up smoking sections, it has become common courtesy at dinner parties to say, "Do you mind if I smoke?" Although nonsmokers may dislike it, you will usually receive gracious permission. However, it is still considered bad form to smoke a pipe at the table during a dinner party.

3. Last year we engaged the services of a man as vice-president of merchandising. He was not a smoker, but he did have the unfortunate habit of chewing gum. Now in all honesty, he was terribly discreet; but there it was, and I was surprised to learn how many of us were annoyed by it. Chewing, like smoking, is a habit—but gum chewing is an easy habit to break.

4. Kleenex was marketed as having two major functions: (*a*) to prevent you from reinfecting yourself by using a handkerchief when you have a cold, and (*b*) to prevent towels from being discolored when removing makeup. Kleenex was *too* successful, and many men now use tissues instead of handkerchiefs for every-day use. Remember, however, that a fresh handkerchief projects a quite different image. It is the mark of a person well born and well bred.

5. Before leaving for lunch, or any kind of meeting, take a few minutes to wash your hands (sticky fingers and dirty fingernails are a turn off), comb your hair, straighten your tie, check for details.

6. When entertaining clients at lunch, it is customary to ask if they would like a cocktail. You would improve your own image, however, if you joined them with a glass of mineral water. Your clients may not be able to "kick the habit" themselves, but they'll think more highly of you if you don't have the habit. You can avoid seeming sanctimonious by pointing out that a drink at lunchtime puts you to sleep. Clients may find you're fun to drink with, but not necessarily the best man to handle their account.

7. When lunching with clients, avoid dishes that will splash on your suit and tie, such as spaghetti. Avoid garlic and onions unless you are on a holiday in the Maine woods.

8. Gambling is absolutely *verboten* with a client. If he loses money . . . you know the rest.

9. Have a good repertoire of interesting anecdotes, mainly light jokes. The four-letter jokes will offend a certain percentage of people, so why risk it?

10. Avoid arguments about politics and/or religion. It is better to lose an argument than to lose an account.

11. Give thought to whom you will invite to a meeting. The presence of too many underlings may create the impression in clients or superiors that you can't handle the situation yourself, and clients don't always want an audience at a meeting.

172

12. When attending meetings, don't grab someone else's usual seat. If there is no established seating, it's customary for senior executives to be seated first.

13. If there are several people from your office calling on a client, it is certainly permissible for all to engage in conversation. If you are making a presentation, however, make sure you coordinate in advance who is going to say what and who is going to respond to which questions.

14. Extend common courtesy to visitors. Offer coffee, have ashtrays available, stand up and greet anyone visiting you with an appointment.

15. Thoughtful gestures are more important to your clients than compromising gifts.

16. Dress consistently—even if you do not have a meeting with a client. You should always be well turned out. It should not be necessary to dress up for important meetings. You should always feel that you look your "business best."

17. What's important to someone else may not be important to you, but consider the other person's feelings. So don't put off things that are easily and quickly taken care of.

18. Patience is a virtue, but it's not always easy. It is desirable to praise people for their contributions to the overall pattern of business, no matter how small.

19. "Please" and "Thank you" to everyone—your own office staff, clients, and their employees.

20. Office affairs are an absolute no-no. Without exception, they lead to wrack and ruin.

21. Be friendly but never intimate with office personnel and avoid situations that could prove to be embarrassing—cocktails after work, candlelight dinners, etc.

22. When greeting a business acquaintance or upon being introduced, a firm handshake tells a lot about a person. Avoid a limp handshake and avoid having sticky fingers. Actually "feel" the

other person's hand and always, always look at him/her and smile. Nothing signals insecurity or shyness more than dropping eyes or failing to smile when introduced.

23. Be aware of your voice and don't be too loud. Four-letter words may signal a common touch, but sometimes they have a reverse effect and people think of you as actually *being* common.

24. Avoid running words together (a mannerism of the 1960s) or speaking too fast. There is an easy way to give your speech greater presence. Place an invisible comma after each word:

> "If, I, place, an invisible, comma, after, each, word; and,
> an invisible, semicolon, after, some, words; my, speech,
> will, have, presence."

Practice saying this sentence slowly out loud until you get the same rhythm used by television newscasters. Listen carefully. Each word is complete and separated from the next word—the invisible comma makes what you say seem more important.

25. Because of the "screw them all" attitude of college students in the 1960s, there has developed a group of men who lack finesse at the table. It is surprising to find college-educated men bringing their mouths down to the food (peasant style) instead of bringing food up to the mouth. It is also surprising that despite all the travel to Europe, most men still eat in the old-fashioned American style: cut the food, drop the knife, switch the fork to the other hand, and bring fork to the mouth then repeat the process. Europeans have a simpler approach—one that in my opinion is easier and more attractive to watch. Rather than describe it, which might be a little difficult, I suggest that the next time you go to a better restaurant, keep your eyes open; you will see the difference.

26. It is not unusual to worry about which knife and fork to use when you are confronted with an array of silverware at a dinner party. Actually, this should present no problem. For starters, you can always follow your hostess. But you will be more comfortable if you know the rules, which are very simple. The forks are on the left, the knives and soup spoons on the right. Utensils for dessert

are placed across the top. If your table has been properly set, you just work from the outside to the inside.

27. When buttering bread, keep the bread on the plate; don't have it in the palm of your hand while you smack the butter about. When you have completed your meal, the knife and fork should be on your plate parallel to each other, with the tines of the fork down. Toothpicks and mobsters go hand in hand. If you have an annoying problem, carry "stim-u-dents" (see Chapter 20) and wait until you are in the privacy of your own office, or the nearest washroom.

28. Place an outdoor thermometer outside your bedroom window so that at the very least, you can start every day properly dressed for the weather.

29. It is customary to remove one's hat when riding in an elevator with ladies. However, it is not necessary to remove one's hat when inside a building.

There is frequent confusion in elevator etiquette about letting women off first. If the elevator is crowded, it is easier to disembark in the natural order. Trying to let women out first holds up the procedure.

30. In certain offices, removing one's jacket may undermine authority.

31. I have one friend, Martin E. Segal, a 5'3" giant both as an investment banker and as a leader in the development of New York City's cultural life. Marty is not only meticulously groomed, but also has established a look of his own. My look is a bow tie and a bowler hat. In his case, it's a fresh red rosebud in the lapel of every suit he wears.

And that's about it for miscellaneous tips, so let's look at a few tips on how to prolong your life.

22

Keep Your Shape in Shape

ALTHOUGH the book market is flooded with diet books and physical fitness books, my suggestions for projecting an image of competence would not be complete without a word about your figure.

Obviously, you can have clothes tailor-made to fit any size or shape, but a career man should give some attention to the shape he's in. Avoid overeating and overdrinking, and get some form of regular exercise.

Since I have had a lifelong battle of the bulge (winning it most of the time), I have accumulated a few tips that may be helpful, both for weight control and overall physical fitness:

1. When I don't have a business luncheon, I always eat a bowl of yogurt with cereal or fruit. Yogurt is an excellent health food and is both nutritious and low in calories. At a business lunch I restrict myself to salad or fish—bread and dessert are out.

2. I avoid cocktails entirely—wine only when we have guests, and then I restrict myself to one glass.

3. The scale is your most truthful friend—get on it every morning. If you've put on two pounds, restrict your calorie intake so that you lose them quickly. Let your doctor establish the ideal weight for your age and figure, and don't get above it.

4. The habit of snacking before going to bed is absolute death. If you have it, break it. If you don't have it, don't get it.

5. Second helpings are out.

6. Eat desserts after dinner, because you deserve it; but make your dessert light (grapefruit, melon) and have only one helping.

7. I take a nap every day before dinner so that I can get two days for the price of one. I end my "daytime day" with a half-hour nap and start my "nighttime day" fully rested.

8. If regular exercise is boring, walk whenever you can. Doctors are agreed that other than swimming, there is no better (or safer) exercise. If jogging is too time-consuming, try ten sit-ups in front of the morning news on TV. According to my doctor, ten sit-ups daily will *prevent* a pot belly from developing, and it's well worth the effort.

9. Eat a good breakfast (protein; no cake or sugar) and, in general, do not skip meals.

Remember that you are (unfortunately) judged by the way you look. A man who watches his figure does have a sense of pride in the way he looks. Moreover, he carries himself better, feels better and, according to my doctor, lives longer. And finally, it *is* better to look better.

Epitaph—Because Every Road Has an Ending

HAVING finished our 22-chapter trip together, you can save yourself some of the time needed for a review by following two suggestions:

1. Try each of the four golden rules, *exactly* as written, before discarding any one.
2. Try every color combination listed in Chapter 8 to see how each one looks on you.

I had a very hard time finding photographs of executives who looked as good as they are. That is, it was difficult to find, on paper, executives who projected the image an executive should project. There is no denying the competence of an executive. He couldn't become a chief executive unless he had what it takes; however, his competence is evidenced by the way in which he says things and the way he does things. It is not usually evidenced, unfortunately, by the way he looks. It is easy to find bad examples, not easy to find good examples, but I managed to scrape together four pictures of chief executives who look the part: Irving Shapiro, Chairman, Du Pont; Bill Bernbach, Chairman, Doyle, Dane, Bernbach; Oscar Kolin, Chairman, Helena Rubinstein; and David Mahoney, Chairman, Norton Simon. I even managed to scrape up a fifth example when Woody Allen, in an effort to cooperate with his public relations counsel, permitted his costume designer to dress him up for what he might consider a "cheesecake" shot.

You may think I take this subject too seriously—not so! For me it's been great fun and I enjoy the fact that I have seen impressive results hundreds and hundreds of times. It really is easy and it really does work. If the men at the very top have some of the many problems indicated in the foregoing pages, then it must be equally true of men on the way up. If anything I have written should prove helpful, then I feel that our time together has been well spent.

When *The New York Times* interviewed me in 1973 for its spotlight article in the financial section of its Sunday edition, the caption read:

LEVITT IS NO STUFFED SHIRT

Not bad for an epitaph—so, I'm asking the executors of my estate to substitute *was* for *is*.

It is easy to find bad examples, but hard to find examples of executives who project the image of an executive. I found four: (TOP LEFT) *Irving Shapiro, Chairman, duPont;* (TOP RIGHT) *Bill Bernbach, Chairman, Doyle, Dane, Bernbach;* (BOTTOM LEFT) *Oscar Kolin, Chairman, Helena Rubinstein, and David Mahoney, Chairman, Norton Simon, Inc.*

Woody Allen makes an all-out effort to project the image of a movie star.

MORTIMER LEVITT opened his first Custom Shop in 1937 and is still the sole owner of the nation-wide chain. He has produced plays, films, and television features and is involved in many cultural and philanthropic activities. He is a founding member of the Manhattan Theater Club and the Levitt Pavillion in Westport, Connecticut, board chairman of the Young Concert Artists, board member of Lincoln Center's Film Society and former board chairman of Daytop Village's drug rehabilitation centers. He is an avid skier, tennis player, sailor and pianist, and lives with his wife, Mimi, in New York City and Westport.